It Happened In Series

IT HAPPENED IN
MAINE

Gail Underwood Parker

TWODOT®

GUILFORD, CONNECTICUT
HELENA, MONTANA
AN IMPRINT OF THE GLOBE PEQUOT PRESS

A · T W O D O T® · B O O K

Copyright © 2004 Morris Book Publishing, LLC

TwoDot is a registered trademark of Morris Book Publishing, LLC.

Map by Stefanie Ward © Morris Book Publishing, LLC

Library of Congress Cataloging-in-Publication Data

Parker, Gail Underwood.
   It happened in Maine / Gail Underwood Parker.— 1st ed.
      p. cm. — (It happened in series)
   Includes bibliographical references and index.
   ISBN-13: 978-0-7627-2733-9
   ISBN-10: 0-7627-2733-0
      1. Maine—History—Anecdotes. I. Title. II. Series.
F19.6.P36 2004
974.1—dc22

                                        2004048226

Manufactured in the United States of America
First Edition/Fifth Printing

To my parents—for their abiding faith and love; and to my former Cape Elizabeth students—some of the historians, writers, and compassionate citizens of our future.

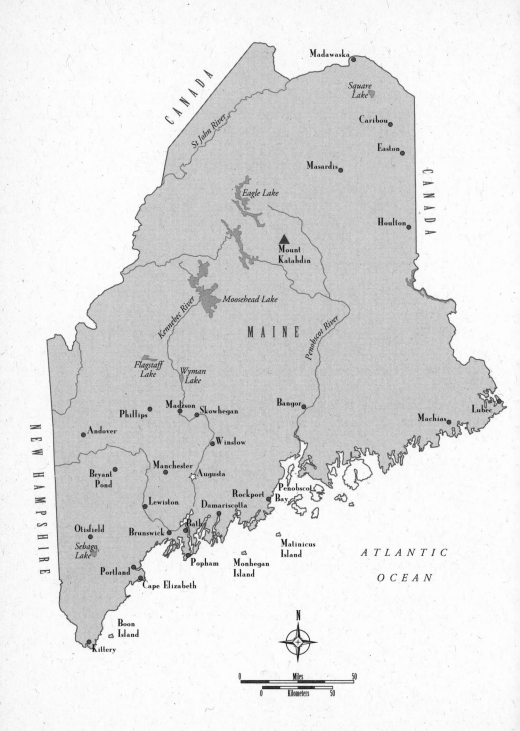

Contents

Preface vii

Acknowledgments ix

The Forgotten Colony—1607 1

Without a Fire—1710 7

A Small Town Fights Back—1775 13

The *Boxer* and the *Enterprise*—1813 18

The Bloodless War—1839 23

Race through the Snow:
    John Poor's Ride to Win a Railway—1845 29

The Start of a Habit—1848 35

The Vision That Began a War—1851 41

Lighthouse Teen—1856 46

Desolation! Desolation!—1866 51

Out of the Ashes—1866 56

The Hunt for a Prize—1897 61

A Sucker Every Minute—1898 66

Maine Women Make Their Mark—1920 72

Off the Trail—1939 77

Silent Night—1944 82

Cheating the Sea: The Wreck of the
    Oakey L. Alexander—1947 87

CONTENTS

In This Corner . . .—1965 93

The Last Log Drive—1976 99

The Seal of Approval: A Governor's Quest—1979 103

And a Child Shall Lead—1983 109

Progress on the Line—1983 115

Justice Delayed—2002 121

Seeds for a Miracle—2003 126

A Potpourri of Maine Facts. 132

A Medley of Maine "Firsts". 136

Bibliography 139

Index 143

About the Author. 147

Preface

Although I have lived in Maine almost thirty-five years, by Maine standards I will always be "from away." But Maine has become the home of my heart as well as my place of residence, so I was excited by the opportunity to explore Maine's history. Readers who know Maine will find some stories familiar, some unexpected. Do you know how Maine became the chewing gum capital of the world, or which governor competed with a seal for headlines? You may find inspiration in the actions of young Hannah Weston, Abbie Burgess, Donn Fendler, and Samantha Smith, or laugh at Prescott Jernegan's $100,000 hoax. Struggle with the crews of the *Oakey Alexander* and the USS *Eagle*. Celebrate an unusual Christmas exchange. There are stories of sacrifice and resilience, of oceans, mountains, and brutal Maine winters. They honor the imagination, determination, and character that have helped make Maine unique.

It Happened in Maine begins with the 1607 Popham Colony, because most earlier stories lack the detailed documentation needed for a full chapter. The stories of early Maine cultures, such as the Oyster Men and Red Paint People, are built on scattered, uncovered artifacts, leaving more questions than answers. The journals of European explorers are among the earliest written records we have of Maine, however cryptic the notes. Early colonists also kept journals and sent reports to their financial backers. Those writings gave me a glimpse into that first colony and its story. The wilderness and weather that challenged Popham can still be experienced in parts of Maine. The story of the Popham colonists is the first of twenty-four stories gathered from the activities of Maine men and women, young and old, who played a part in the events that shaped and gave personality to Maine for almost three hundred years.

Through these stories the people and Maine's past come alive. Maine has so many wonderful stories that the challenge of writing this book was how to decide which were the very best. *It Happened in Maine* has twenty-four stories I couldn't resist. I hope you enjoy them. There are many others to be found. I leave it to you to explore them on your own. Happy hunting!

Acknowledgments

All my life I have been curious. My parents, James and Ethel Underwood, always encouraged my curiosity and pointed me in the right direction to find the answers to puzzling questions myself. Growing up, I discovered that when you find the answer to one question, it often makes you think of another question, and another, and another. *It Happened in Maine* will answer some questions, but should make you think of new ones. I hope it makes you curious enough to look for answers yourself. Before you know it, you too may be hooked on the fabulous scavenger hunt that is called research. In the process you may learn that history is full of excitement, humor, and the drama of real people and real stories.

Some of the many people I thank for helping explore some of the stories in Maine's history are:

—the staff of the Maine Historical Society library.

—volunteers at the Phillips Historical Society, the Margaret Chase Smith Library, the Madawaska Public Library, and the Portland Fire Museum who opened their doors and patiently answered many questions.

—Buster Violette, Janet Fletcher, Lorraine Luttrell, Bobbie Gottschalk, Julia Hunter, Betty Montgomery, Michael Hathaway, and Elsie Dill for sharing their memories and their lives.

—Ann, Kathy, and Cathy at the Portland Public Library, who helped as I waded through thousands of microfilmed newspapers; Tom Gaffney and the staff at the Portland Room who helped me locate old documents and records.

—Bud Warren, John Bradford, and Bobbie Gottschalk, who reviewed specific chapters, and Bill Barry, who reviewed the finished manuscript.

—Gwilyum Roberts, Bill Greene, Herb Adams, and Marty Watts who allowed me to pick their brains about stories from Maine's past worth tracking down.

I would never have had the opportunity to work on this project had not Megan Hiller first remembered an unusual cookbook proposal and suggested me to Charlene Patterson for this book, then later shepherded the book through to completion. Thanks, too, for supporting the idea of including a reference map for readers.

Thanks also go to Carolyn Yoder and the gang at the Highlights workshop for their early encouragement and feedback; to my Brunswick writers group: Cindy, Robin, Sue, Anna, and Katie, for their continued moral support and suggestions; to friends Ruth Clark and Bev Bisbee for willingly listening to a new discovery and sympathizing with a dead end; to the gang at Romeo's Pizza who let me type for hours in the back booth, nibbling on a BLT; to Alexis, Jen, and Rachel, who babysat so that I could go to interviews or on research trips; and to Sasha, Shawn, Eric, and Mariah, who put up with babysitters and picked-up dinners writing nights. Thanks also to Tracy, Robin, Ernie, and so many others, who always asked how "The Book" was coming and in doing so helped keep it going. Special thanks to Hayden Atwood for being patient with my grammatical lapses, and for being as generous with his encouragement as with his pencil.

Thank you to those special colleagues who have given me moral support through a challenging transition from teacher to writer. Thank you also to each of the amazing students and parents of my 2001–2002 fifth-grade class who made my last year of teaching the most precious and wonderful year, especially for adding such surprises and happy memories to the last week, and to Joe Kearney for being part of that year's strength and the surprise.

Most important, like my father, my grown daughters Leah, Miriam, Anna, Alexis, and Belinda, have never failed to believe in my writing projects and always have helped make it possible for me to write. On this project Miriam became my indispensable right hand, helping me keep each story focused and always challenging me with her keen ear for the story and the writing.

The Forgotten Colony

· 1607 ·

Gathered around the small field on Sabino Head, a hundred men listened to the sermon delivered by chaplain Richard Seymour. Next the charter was read and the leaders named: George Popham, president; Raleigh Gilbert, second in command; and others. A reading of the laws to be observed completed the special service. It was August 19, 1607, and the Virginia Company of England was taking formal possession of what is now New England. The Northern Colony of Virginia was begun.

England's King James I had chartered the Virginia Company to settle the east coast of North America based on claims resulting from John Cabot's explorations. A group of investors from London was granted the southern region—Cape Fear, North Carolina, to the Potomac River. They had sent colonists a few months earlier to establish a colony at Jamestown. A group of investors from the Plymouth area of Devon was granted the northern region—Long Island to New Brunswick. Whichever was more successful settling their region would gain the land between. Sir John Popham, Lord Chief Justice of England, became the principal investor for the northern colony. His nephew, George, would lead the colony.

The colonists had sailed from Plymouth, England, on May 31, in the *Gift of God* and the *Mary and John*. Separated during the long voyage, the two ships regrouped off Pemaquid. Arriving at Sagadahoc in mid-August, they chose Sabino's rocky cliff and grassy field for their new home. The service made the colony official.

The next morning, the work of building Fort Saint George began. Dividing up, one group began digging a trench for the outer fortification, a traditional star fort modified to fit the geography of the headland. The men discovered rocky glacial remnants after digging just a few feet down. So they dug a trench 20 feet wide, piling up the dirt to build a rampart. Other men gathered bundles of sticks to reinforce the rampart. When completed, cannons would be placed on its top to protect the settlement.

Another team began work on the all-important storehouse, where supplies would be kept for the winter. The storehouse was timber frame, built in a series of roughly 10-foot bays, two deep and seven long inside the fort's west wall. One group cleared the ground for the earthen floor, while others began digging holes 3 feet in diameter for the wall posts. Pine was cut into wall posts a foot on each side. After raising the posts into the holes, earth was packed tightly around in the familiar earth-fast, post-and-beam construction.

When the posts were up, wall studs were set into sills formed between each set of posts. Walls were made of "wattle and daub," thin strips of wood packed and sealed with a daub thickened with grasses and small twigs. A tough grassy plant growing all around the settlement provided thatch for the roof.

Bay by bay the storehouse took shape. By September 9, the men had made enough progress on the storehouse to begin unloading supplies. Simple white glass beads, earthenware, and trading goods went into one section. Dry and preserved foodstuffs went into another. Iron hardware, lead balls, and shot went into a section to be used as the armory. On October 8, after all the cases, tools, and supplies had been unloaded, the *Mary and John* sailed for England.

On board the *Mary and John* was draftsman John Hunt, probably a military cartographer, who carried back a precious paper map. Using a scale of feet and paces, Hunt had carefully marked each building's location, sketching a profile and labeling its use. The meticulously drawn map of Fort Saint George was a mix of what was complete and what was planned, even marking the spot for a garden.

But there wasn't time for a garden yet. After the 19-by-70-foot storehouse was completed, work began on Raleigh Gilbert's house. With much left to be built, the colonists shifted to more primitive, but faster, construction, using Y-shaped crotchet posts to support the rafters. A stone hearth and chimney were the most challenging features of Gilbert's home. Time was growing short and the weather was deteriorating. Simple buildings, little more than shelters, may have been hastily constructed for the colonists and their work, but not all of the planned buildings were completed.

While the construction continued, the leaders worked toward making the colony profitable. A few went up the river to explore the area's resources and trade with the natives. Reports sent to England cite a wide variety of assets the colony offered: "multitude of goodlye Rivers & harbourse it doth abound with all" and "fish in the season, in great plenty . . . mastidge for shipps, goodly Oakes, and Ceaders, with infinite sortes of trees." They even acknowledged the colony to the north at Saint Croix, describing "rich Furrs if they can keepe the Frenchmen from the trade."

A daily journal attributed to colonist Robert Davies described the area: "Illands are all overgrowen with woods very thicke as ocks wallnyut pyne trees & many other things growinge as Sarsaperilla hassellnnyts & whorts in abundance."

According to the Davies journal, not everyone was working on the buildings or scouting resources. The ship carpenters had begun building a ship for the colony's use. A London shipwright named Digby was in charge and built what was described as a "pretty pinnace of about 30 tonne." This was no kit boat brought from home and assembled on site. This ship was built from scratch in the new colony. Area trees provided the wood, and ship carpenters used an iron caulking tool to fit pitch-coated oakum into the cracks between planks. The coated fibers sealed each joint and waterproofed the hull. Although the ship was not finished until after Hunt sailed back to England, Hunt optimistically drew it on his map, at full sail off the colony.

The winter was filled with disappointments, disasters, and unexpected cold. Although the latitude was similar to England's, the weather and winds were far more bitter than at home. After a mid-December meeting of the ruling council at the admiral's house, the colony decided that half the men would return to England on the *Gift of God*. In February the colony's president, George Popham, died, leaving the younger, rougher, and inexperienced Raleigh Gilbert in charge of the forty-five remaining colonists. Relationships with the natives were not as useful as had been hoped, no usable mines had been found, and the fur trade was also not as good as had been hoped.

Sir John Popham, the colony's financial backer, had pledged 500 pounds per year for five years to support the venture. This would pay for the supplies needed by the colonists until the colony was profitable. Two supply ships left England for Fort Saint George in late March. In addition to supplies they may have brought very bad news. Sir John Popham had died.

When the *Mary and John* returned to the colony in early September, it brought startling news for Raleigh Gilbert. His older brother, Sir John Gilbert, had died, leaving Raleigh the heir to the family title and land. The struggling Popham colony already had lost its president and its financial backing. It had not yet established the expected profitable trade. Now its current leader could have wealth and status by simply returning to England. Whatever the combination of reasons, within a month everything was loaded onto the colony-built pinnace *Virginia* and the *Mary and John*. The colony that had begun with the optimism and determination of the August ceremony ended after only thirteen months, in September 1608.

The colony at present-day Popham, Maine, did not struggle with starvation or near mutiny as did its sister colony in Jamestown. Popham never achieved financial success or long-term settlement. The fame and glory of a permanent New England settlement would wait more than a decade for the Plymouth colonists. But Popham is making its own valuable contribution to history. The very abandonment of Popham, which labeled it a failure, enables it to be a success today. Because the site was occupied for only that single year, it's like a time capsule. The artifacts and evidence at the site give experts a precise time slice to study. Hunt's map is the only pictorial record we have to show how the English built their early settlements.

Supported by a team of assistants and volunteers, Dr. Jeffrey Brain, an archaeologist with the Peabody Essex Museum, has been working for a decade to unravel the mysteries of Popham. First learning of it while visiting friends, Brain became hooked by stories of the little-known colony. Steady research and repeated excavations have shed light on what Fort Saint George was like.

The first evidence of the storehouse was unearthed in 1994, when Dr. Brain's team found the rotted remains of one of the storehouse posts. Since then, Dr. Brain's teams have uncovered bottle glass, buttons, North Devon ceramics, Bellarmine stoneware, musket balls, and even plate armor fragments from the colony. Hunt's map has been invaluable as they work to unearth proof of the buildings, post by post, and document the colony forgotten over time. Wood fragments, stained soil, and carefully laid stone hearths and sills, uncovered after nearly 400 years, testify to the efforts of that brave group of men. Popham's Fort Saint George failed financially, but it gives witness to the men's courage, daring unknown elements to explore and settle a new land.

NOTE: The building of the *Virginia* by the Popham colonists began a long tradition of Maine shipbuilding. In the 400 years since, over five thousand wooden and steel ships have been launched on the same Kennebec River. The sturdy, deepwater ship *Virginia* helped carry the colonists back to England and recrossed the Atlantic a year later to the sister colony in Jamestown. Plans are underway in Maine to build a thirty-ton pinnace based on the original *Virginia*. The research and design work is complete. The project, called "Maine's First Ship," hopes to build and launch her in time to celebrate the 400th anniversary of the Popham colony's founding. Traveling educational programs aboard the new *Virginia* will commemorate the colony and the start of Maine's maritime heritage.

Without a Fire
·1710·

Captain John Deane and the *Nottingham Galley* left London, England, on August 2, 1710, loaded with cordage. They then stopped in Killybegs, Ireland, adding thirty tons of butter, over 300 cheeses, and other stores before heading for Boston on September 25. The 120-ton British merchant ship carried ten guns and a crew of thirteen. Ship's Mate Christopher Langman later claimed the ship and crew were in no fit condition for a transatlantic voyage, saying that "4 of the Guns were useless, and that not above 6 of the Men were capable to Serve in the Ship, in case of bad Weather."

The crossing proved difficult, but in early December the *Nottingham Galley* briefly sighted land before being swallowed by fog as it approached the coast of New England. Around eight or nine o'clock on the night of December 11, the ship suddenly rammed a rocky shoal and immediately began to break apart. Sighting a dark shape a little off from the ship, the crew swam for the safety of land. In a short time all fourteen crawled ashore, relieved to survive the wreck. Langman later described their despair as they surveyed their surroundings:

> When we got ashore we found it to be a desolate small island, without any Shelter; and being wet, and having but few Clothes, some began to despair of being able to live there till the Morning; and besides, we were not certain but it might be over flow'd at high Tide . . . we expected to perish there.

Huddling together, the men did make it through the night and in the morning explored their haven. It didn't take long. At normal high tide Boon Island measures fewer than 150 feet by 300 feet, smaller than a regulation football field. More frightening, the island's highest point was a mere 14 feet above the ocean's crashing waves. Everyone knew the severe storm tides could submerge the entire island. Worse was its barrenness. In 1876, 156 years later, lightkeeper's daughter Annie Bell Hobbs described Boon Island: "The island is made up of nothing but rocks, without one foot of ground for trees, shrubs, or grass." There would be no shelter made from tree boughs, no wild game caught for food, no wood for a signal fire.

The men scoured the rocky shore for anything washed up from the *Nottingham Galley,* but precious little was found. Rigging a rough tentlike shelter from a scrap of sail, the men slept on top of each other to conserve body warmth in the freezing December cold. The next day, three cheeses washed ashore, which Deane described as "beaten into uncouth Forms by the violent Dashing of the Sea against the Rock." A few beef bones were found and "render'd eatable by pounding on the Rock." They found that the seaweed was edible, and low tide uncovered mussels on the rocks. The only good fortune was plentiful water. Snow and rain collected in the many hollows and crevices created by years of wave action on the rocky ledges. The salt spray made the water foul at lower points, but the hollows on higher ground held quite usable water.

When the weather cleared, the men saw how close to safety they had come. York beach was visible just a few miles away, with ships sailing in and out of the harbor, but they had no way to make themselves seen at that distance.

The ship's cook died of exposure on the third or fourth day; his body was taken to the shore at low tide, and high tide carried it away. The men desperately needed warmth and hope if they were to survive. As waves continued to pound the *Nottingham Galley*'s remains, a few more precious items washed up. The men rescued a second piece of canvas, triangular in shape and almost 10 feet across. They used it to make a better shelter from the howling wind and topped it with a white distress flag, still hoping for rescue.

A caulking mallet, hammer, cutlass blade, and bits of wood with nails also washed up. Their best hope was to get help themselves, so the men began to shape a rough boat. There were only nine to ten hours of daylight per day and little warmth from the December sun even at its highest. Working on the boat exposed them to the elements, and some would stay in the shelter to conserve warmth. And as Langman later explained: "[N]or could we walk on the Rock in order to keep us warm, it was so craggy, uneven and slippery."

The seaweed worked fairly well for food, but the mussels did not. For a few days each man got six or seven of them after harvesting at low tide, but soon the shellfish caused painful cramps and were abandoned. During the second week a seagull was found in a hole in the rocks and was killed. The raw meat was welcome, but one bird would not prevent starvation for a dozen men. They kept working.

The boat was finished by December 21; its bottom was three planks wide, the side half a plank high, with a small square sail on the short mast. The half-dozen strongest men would use short, roughly shaped paddles and one longer steering paddle to navigate the miles between their island and the mainland. Eagerly, the men pushed the boat into the surf and prepared to climb in, but the boat broke apart on the rocks before even clearing the surf around the shoals. Struggling back through the icy water to the relative safety of Boon Island, the men sat watching the boat's remnants float away. That afternoon, a fresh storm blew in, and they comforted themselves that the makeshift boat could never have survived the trip in the storm.

Not willing to give in to despair, a Scandinavian sailor led the effort to build a raft from the little wood they had left.

Despite frostbitten hands and feet, a few of the sailors began to fashion a two-person raft. Many of the men were in such bad shape that they were unable to help. In addition to cold and hunger, the men now suffered from boils, ulcers, and peeling skin around the legs and ankles of those who still had boots. The ship's carpenter was in the worst shape. Around forty-seven years old and overweight, he had been failing steadily. He died around Christmas Day, and his body was taken out of the shelter. The crew had been shipwrecked for over two weeks with only morsels of food, little shelter, and no heat at all.

The ten still alive were desperate. Though Langman's and Deane's later accounts of the ordeal vary in the details, both acknowledge the despair, which drove them to use the carpenter's body as food. Deane recalled: "A few thin Slices, wash'd in Salt-water, were brought into the Tent, and given to every one, with a good Quantity of Rockweed to supply the Place of Bread." The distasteful choice fed their bodies but left their souls with an added burden. In his later published account Captain Deane described the state of the men as New Year's Day approached:

> half frozen, more than half famished, distempered,
> ulcerous, despairing, unable to help themselves . . .
> in a Word, labouring under a Complication of the
> greatest Evils, Colds, Diseases, Famine, Prospect of
> Death, and—Dread of Damnation.

Work continued on the raft and finally it was done. The Scandinavian and another strong swimmer pushed it out into the surf and made it through the first breakers. Suddenly, it was caught by a wave and overturned, almost drowning the two. The second sailor was too shaken to try again, but another stepped forward and joined the Scandinavian. Together they steered the raft through the surf. Their shipmates on the island waved them encouragement and watched the small craft's progress perhaps halfway to the mainland when the sun set and they could no longer see its tiny shape. As days passed with no rescue, hope that their shipmates had reached shore disappeared.

Several of the men experienced convulsions, and one had "essentially lost his mind," when Deane crawled from the makeshift shelter on the morning of January 2 and saw a small open boat. Less than 3 miles away, it was heading directly for the island. Remembering that moment, he said that "the Prospect of so sudden and unexpected a Deliverance, outstrips the Powers of Tongue and Mind."

Neither of the men on the raft had survived, but the body of the second sailor had washed ashore, frozen, with an oar strapped to his wrist. Searchers discovered the remains of the raft less than a mile away and set out in a shallop to search nearby islands for an explanation.

Not expecting to find survivors, the rescuers were using a boat too small to bring them to shore. They left a small canoe for the survivors to burn for warmth and headed back to the mainland for help. After twenty-two days the survivors finally had a fire and struggled to get warm as they waited for the rescue they knew was coming. A brief storm delayed the return, but on January 4 a larger shallop arrived. A canoe carried a couple of survivors at a time from Boon Island. Langman recalled the difficulty: "[S]everal of us had our Legs so frozen, and were so weak that we could not walk." In two hours all were safe aboard and by evening they were ashore. For the first time in twenty-four days, the survivors of the *Nottingham Galley* were fed, clothed, and warm.

In June 1995 underwater archaeologist Warren Riess raised a cannon from 25 feet of water near the jagged, rocky shoals that had doomed the ship 275 years earlier. Looking at the island, which is barely more than a pile of rocks, he marveled at the "miracle of tenacity and ability" that any survived in the dead of winter without food or fire. Most of the men lost fingers and toes to frostbite, one a foot. Ship's Mate Langman and Captain Deane both published detailed accounts of the ordeal. Some went back to sea. All carried scars, both physical and emotional, of their twenty-four day nightmare. They had made choices that seem impossible to most, but they survived the ravages of wind, cold, hunger, and despair, and thanks to the sacrifices of their shipmates, the ten remaining crew of the *Nottingham Galley* were rescued.

A Small Town Fights Back
·1775·

When Lexington and Concord stood up to British troops in April 1775, a spirit of defiance spread up and down New England. In the Province of Maine, the tiny villages of Machias and nearby Chandler's River (now Jonesboro) heard about the fighting. Machias had been successfully settled by the English just twelve years earlier, but the British oppression offended the colonists. The men of Machias met at Burnham's Tavern to discuss options for resisting the English. After the meeting they cut down a towering pine and brought it to the center of the village. With everyone cheering they raised Maine's first official liberty pole. The straight, tall pole, still topped with green, was a sign of local support for the independence movement. The Machias Sons of Liberty immediately formed a company of minutemen. Jeremiah O'Brien was one of its leaders.

Lumber from the rich Machias forests was shipped all over New England. That June, Boston trader Ichabod Jones proposed bringing up a shipload of supplies Machias needed. In payment Machias would provide a load of lumber Jones could sell in Boston. Jones was loyal to the British, and he knew that feeling was running high against Loyalists in many parts of New England. He arranged an escort for his ships, the *Unity* and the *Polly*. An armed British schooner, the *Margaretta,* would offer protection. The *Margaretta*'s twenty-man crew was led by a brash, twenty-five-year-old British midshipman named James Moore.

On Friday, June 2, the ships sailed into Machias Harbor. Moore was outraged by the town's liberty pole. He would not unload the town's supplies until the pole was taken down and the lumber loaded. The town refused. The wood was intended to build barracks for the increasing number of unwanted British troops garrisoned in Boston. Knowing this made the colonists even more reluctant to supply the lumber. For a week there was a standoff.

On Saturday, June 10, the men of Machias met at O'Brien's Brook to decide what to do. Legend says the discussion went round and round with no sign of a decision. Finally, old Colonel Benjamin Foster got tired of all the talking. Exhorting his fellow townsmen to take a stand, he stepped dramatically across the brook. He challenged those in favor of taking action against the British to step across and join him. One by one, every single man did.

The men devised a plan to capture the British officers and get their supplies from the ships. On Sunday morning, June 11, they closed in while the officers attended church services. Moore and several others escaped out a church window. They made it back to the *Margaretta* and an uneasy quiet settled over the town and harbor.

Word went out to neighboring settlements that Machias desperately needed all able-bodied men to bring their arms and help defend the village against the expected attack from the British ship. About twenty men from Chandler's River headed immediately for Machias. Taking what little ammunition they had, they urged the town's women to scour the settlement for more and send it to Machias. There was no real road between the settlements, not even a set path. The men cut notches in trees, marking their trail through the 16 miles of dense wilderness between the two settlements.

In Chandler's River two young girls gathered supplies for

making ammunition. Hannah and Rebecca Weston were sisters-in-law, just nineteen and seventeen years old. They hurried from house to house asking for lead and powder. Knowing the danger facing Machias, women even gave their precious pewter spoons to be melted down into musket balls. Hannah and Rebecca gathered almost forty pounds of shot, powder, and pewter and packed them into a pillowcase.

With all the healthy men already gone to Machias, there was no one else willing to take the supplies there. Hannah and Rebecca volunteered. Taking meat and bread, the pillowcase, and a small hatchet, they began the 16-mile journey alone. Hannah and Rebecca soon struggled with the weight of the ammunition, the difficulty of the rough terrain, and the lack of a trail. They crossed brooks and slogged through swamps, occasionally stopping to rest on a fallen tree. The usual noises of the woods were joined by the sound of an occasional wolf or owl. Fighting exhaustion and fear, the girls continued to push toward Machias, still miles ahead.

Back in Machias the men who had gathered were a mix of farmers, sailors, river log drivers, and lumbermen. Armed with an assortment of pitchforks, clubs, axes, and the occasional musket, the three dozen men managed to board and capture the *Unity* and the *Polly,* but they were unable to take command of the *Margaretta.* With only three rounds each remaining in their muskets, the colonists were hopelessly outgunned by the British ship. They hastily built rough shields of thick pine boards to raise around the *Unity*'s deck and waited for Moore to make a move.

Late on June 12, Moore decided to sail the *Margaretta* back to Boston without the lumber, but he ran into trouble leaving Machias Harbor. The faster *Unity* pursued the *Margaretta,* and led by Captain Jeremiah O'Brien, the Machias patriots attacked. Somewhat protected behind the rough pine shield, one of the men on board the *Unity* took careful aim and was able to shoot the helmsman of the *Margaretta.* The *Unity* then rammed the *Margaretta,* her bowsprit ripping the *Margaretta*'s mainsail. Patriots leapt across, boarding the *Margaretta* and grappling hand to hand with the British. At the end of the battle, Moore was fatally wounded, the British flag lowered, and the *Margaretta* in colonial hands. The first naval battle of what would become the American Revolution had been won by the colonists.

Just as night fell, Hannah and Rebecca struggled up a steep hill and saw one of the houses of Machias ahead. On reaching the house they learned that the *Margaretta* had already been captured, but the people of Machias were no less grateful for their efforts in delivering the munition supplies. The supplies were still desperately needed for making ammunition to protect the settlement.

The people of Machias, led by Captain O'Brien and Colonel Foster, congratulated the girls on their "bravery and perseverance" in bringing the ammunition to the village's defense. To honor Hannah and Rebecca, two Machias merchants presented them with 12 yards of the finest "Camlet" cloth. The cloth sold for four shillings per yard, making a total value of two pounds, eight shillings. The two women divided the fabric equally and each made a special dress. The cloth was of much better quality than that of ordinary dresses, and over fifty years later, Hannah Weston still cherished fragments of her "Camlet dress."

Captain O'Brien refitted the British ships for colonial use and shortly thereafter captured another British ship, the *Diligence.* The four ships became the nucleus of a small navy for Massachusetts. They defended the Machias area from retribution and protected much of the coast of the Province of Maine. News of the events at Machias soon reached Philadelphia, where the Continental Congress was debating the feasibility of commissioning a navy to assist the colonial cause. The determination of ordinary citizens, men, women, and even young girls, to defend their rights was impressive. It demonstrated the power of even untrained, barely armed, but motivated civilians. For its first "naval fleet," and first naval battle of the American Revolution, tiny Machias, Maine, is considered the birthplace of the American navy.

The *Boxer* and the *Enterprise*

·1813·

The British brigantine *Boxer* was based in Saint John, New Brunswick, Canada, and carried eighteen guns and a crew of 104. Her commander, Samuel Blyth, had gone to sea at eleven years old and at twenty-nine was eager to command the *Boxer.* He was to keep privateers under control and disrupt New England commerce, especially along the troublesome Maine coast.

Built in 1799, the American brigantine *Enterprise* was unusually fast and had been recently refitted to carry sixteen guns and a 102-man crew. She was commanded by Captain William Burrows, who had recently served on the USS *Constitution*. An eager, skilled captain, also twenty-nine, he had similar instructions to control privateers along Maine's coast.

On September 5, 1813, Americans spotted the *Boxer* chasing a merchant ship toward Bath's harbor. Under full sail the merchant ship raced into the harbor as the *Boxer* fired two shots toward her. Both splashed beyond the ship as she slipped into the safety of the harbor with her cargo. The *Boxer* broke off pursuit. Reports of the *Boxer's* attack reached the *Enterprise,* which immediately began hunting the *Boxer.*

The two ships spotted each other off Monhegan Island around 5:00 A.M. At 7:30 they weighed anchor and fired challenging shots, but as the wind calmed, the two ships were left 4 miles apart, with limp sails, unable to have at each other.

At 11:30 a breeze began, and by afternoon it was strong enough for the two ships to start maneuvering. At 2:15 the *Enterprise* shortened its sails, hoisted its ensign, and fired a fresh challenging shot at the *Boxer.* Each continued tacking to gain the wind's advantage for the coming battle, until at 3:00 the two ships began closing in. Sailors later reported events to the *Eastern Argus,* Portland's newspaper: "At 3:15, The enemy being within half pistol shot gave three cheers and commenced the action by firing her starboard broadside. We then returned them three cheers, with our starboard broadside, when the action became general." The *Boxer*'s Captain Blyth was killed instantly in the first round of fire.

For thirty minutes the two ships raked each other with fire. Captain Burrows was mortally wounded while manning a cannon on deck. Sailors said later, "Our brave commander fell and while lying on the deck refusing to be carried below, raised his head, and requested that the flag might never be struck." All around him shards of broken masts and splinters of blasted gunnels flew through the air. Tangled rigging fell. Sailors on both ships manned their posts until they were cut down by explosions, cannon fire, or falling debris.

Forty-five minutes after the first shot had been fired, the flag still flew over the damaged but victorious *Enterprise.* The *Boxer* was dismasted, riddled with holes, and taking on water. Onboard the *Enterprise* Captain Burrows accepted the sword of the *Boxer*'s commander and finally agreed to be taken below. He died eight hours later.

Two days later, the two ships arrived in Portland. The *Enterprise* had severe hits to the foremast and mainmast; the *Boxer* was barely afloat. Navy Captain Isaac Hull reported the staggering damage:

The Boxer has eighteen or twenty 18-pound shots in her hull, most of them at water's edge; several stands of 18-pound grape stick in her side, and such a quantity of small grape that I did not undertake to count them. Her masts, sails, and spares are literally cut to pieces. I counted in her mainmast alone, three 18-pound shot holes, 18 large grapeshot holes, 16 musket ball holes, and a large number of smaller shot holes without counting about the cat harpins.

Twenty men working at pumps were required to keep the *Boxer* from sinking while docked at Union Wharf. More than two dozen wounded were taken ashore. The *Eastern Argus* proudly reported that "in the care of the wounded there was made no distinction. The British sailor received the same treatment as the American . . . It is a fact worth recording." The same equality applied to the dead, particularly the two captains. On September 8 they were given a joint heroes' funeral and buried with full military honors. The *Eastern Argus* published instructions for the elaborate and solemn ceremonies. The paper also announced, "Military gentlemen are requested to appear in full uniform" and "Shipping in the Harbor will wear their colors at half mast." Their instructions were carried out to the letter.

Portland had only one horse-drawn hearse, but another wagon was hastily painted black and draped so that both mahogany caskets could be carried with appropriate dignity. Two funeral barges, also draped in black, carried the bodies of the two captains from their ships to the shore. Masters called the cadence as mates rowed the ten wrapped and muffled oars of each barge. As they rowed, the *Boxer* and *Enterprise* fired alternating salutes on minute guns. Solemn music was performed by a full band at the wharf as each captain's body was transferred to a hearse and covered with the flag of his ship.

Hundreds of people assembled at the courthouse, following the order published in the *Eastern Argus*. A military escort, municipal leaders, and clergy formed the head of the procession. The casket of Captain Burrows, escorted by specified officers from the *Enterprise,* led the mourners. Each pallbearer was assigned a specific place and the brig's remaining officers and crew followed. Next, the designated officers of the *Boxer* marched alongside Captain Blyth's casket. The other surviving British officers and crew lined up after their captain. Officers of the U.S. Navy, other ranking military, and bank presidents concluded the ranks of dignitaries. Citizens of Portland and the vicinity formed at the rear. At precisely 9:00 A.M., the huge procession headed for the First Parish Meeting House, escorted by the Portland Rifle Company. Bells tolled all across the city in tribute to the fallen commanders.

Following the funeral, artillery companies on Munjoy Hill fired more salutes, echoed by guns at the harbor's Fort Preble and Fort Scammel, as the spectacular procession made its way past the flag-draped Portland Observatory to the Eastern Cemetery. The two young adversaries were buried side by side with equal honors. The *Portland Gazette* praised the crowds that had lined the streets and surrounded the cemetery, reporting that "the highest degree of order prevailed, and solemn silence was kept."

There was no such silence five days later when two celebratory dinners were held. The dinner at Mechanics Hall, near Burnham's Wharf, was for the surviving sailors of the *Enterprise*. Informal and rowdy, it lacked official dignitaries, but not pride. The *Eastern Argus* reported their postdinner toasts. The first wished their old ships always be granted "wind about the beam." But with each round of rum, the American sailors became more blunt. By tradition sailors who drowned were said to be in "Davy's Locker." A later toast reported by the *Argus* was: "To Davy's Locker—may it accommodate all the enemies to free trade and sailor's rights."

The dinner at Union Hall on Free Street was quite different.

More formal and sedate, the commissioned officers of both ships were included. The *Argus* reported on the "Dinner of the Brave Tars":

> [The sailors] marched in procession . . . to the music of an excellent Band, greeted by hazzas of numerous citizens at the corners of streets . . . young, active *enterprizing* fellows with *American* blood in their veins and American Independence in their hearts.

After dinner John Mussey served as toastmaster, with a succession of formal toasts to the president, the governor, and the navy. When men finally rose to toast the fallen, they treated them equally, as had the Portland physicians and the funeral mourners. They toasted the fallen Burrows, the *Enterprise,* and even Blyth and the *Boxer.* "To the conquerors and conquered of the *Boxer,* Enemies by Law, but in gallantry and worth we pronounce them brothers."

Years later, facts emerged suggesting the battle of the *Boxer* and the *Enterprise* need never have happened. The merchant ship that had appeared to barely escape the *Boxer* was loaded with wool blankets and cloth purchased illegally from Canada to fill a merchant's order for blankets and uniforms for American troops. The ship's owners had hired the *Boxer* to provide safe escort from Halifax to Bath. To give the appearance of chasing her, the *Boxer* had deliberately fired the shots over the top of the ship. Sadly, the charade worked all too convincingly. Dozens of sailors and two eager young captains were forever joined, and honored, in death.

The Bloodless War
· 1839 ·

Maine's Governor Edward Kent was angry. Lumbermen from the British territory of New Brunswick, Canada were cutting timber in Maine's Aroostook region again. Kent asked the Maine legislature for a resolution demanding the British abide by the border or face dire consequences. Maine not only was prepared to defend her border, but also to ask assistance from the federal government. Governor Kent made his case to the legislature in January 1838:

> No State is to be left to defend its soil single-handed and alone. It is the duty of a state to claim and assert its rights or jurisdiction, and it is the duty of the general government to protect and maintain them if well founded.

The legislature agreed, insisting if the United States government didn't act, Maine would act on her own. Daniel Webster spoke before Congress, supporting Maine's rights under the Treaty of 1783, and the Committee on Foreign Affairs (chaired by future president James Buchanan) agreed. But after no sign of action, Maine initiated her own review of earlier border surveys. Kent and the legislature considered the British-Canadians to be timber thieves, stealing valuable wood and its profits from Maine. They had to be stopped.

Lumbering had been a key factor in the northern

territories since the first English and French settlers arrived. Even the unforested land was valuable. Unlike the rocky soil in the southern part of the Maine territories, Aroostook farmland was rich and fertile. The border between the Maine territories and New Brunswick was unclear under the Treaty of 1783, leaving both Maine and New Brunswick claiming the Aroostook region. A compromise offered by King William of the Netherlands was accepted by the British government but never by the United States. This was no picky detail of boundaries. The disputed area covered 12,000 square miles, roughly one and one-half times the size of present-day Rhode Island, and a third of Maine's total territory. Neither Maine nor New Brunswick was about to back down. An already tense situation began to escalate.

Governor John Fairfield replaced Kent in January 1839, and later that month he sent a report alerting the legislature to the growing threat along the northern border. Saying that the "character of the state is clearly involved," he urged immediate action. The legislature agreed and ordered land agents to locate, arrest, and jail anyone "trespassing" on state lands.

On February 1, 1839, Maine land agent Rufus McIntire set out for the disputed region. With him were the sheriff of Penobscot County, Major Hastings Strickland, and 200 men, including an Old Town militia company. They built a supply post at Masardis and mounted several cannon at the mouth of the Saint Croix. Farther north they used the iced-over Aroostook River, continuing to the mouth of the Little Madawaska River (where Caribou is today). Warned of the approaching militia, the 200-man British-Canadian lumber crew retreated up the Saint John to Tobique, where they created a stir with their story.

McIntire's militia camped at Little Madawaska the night of February 12, but McIntire and two others continued several miles to what is now Fort Fairfield. He planned to meet with James McLauchlin, New Brunswick's "Warden of the Disputed

Territory," at Fitzherbert's Tavern. When the lumbermen and townspeople in Tobique heard about the planned meeting, an angry mob of fifty men gathered to put an end to Maine's interference. The British-Canadians surrounded the tavern and, after a brief fracas, captured McIntire and the two men. They turned the Americans over to authorities in Woodstock, who sent them by horse-drawn sled to Fredericton, New Brunswick, where the Americans were thrown in jail.

That morning the militia in Little Madawaska heard of McIntire's capture and jailing. Rumors of an attacking British army sent the militia rushing back to the stronger base at Masardis, while Major Strickland hurried to Augusta to inform Governor Fairfield. Fairfield sent New Brunswick's Lieutenant Governor John Harvey a message to "ascertain whether these high-handed proceedings of the Trespassers are authorized . . . and to procure the release of the Agent and those taken with him."

The first hint ordinary Mainers had of trouble brewing was a small paragraph in the *Portland Advertiser* of February 14:

> There is a rumor here this afternoon that the trespassers have organized for resistance to the force that had been sent to arrest them, that they muster three or four hundred . . . I have not been able to trace this report to any authentic source, and only give it to you as one of the rumors of the day.

By February 17 Warden McLauchlin led a British-Canadian contingent to the Masardis base. He told the Maine militia that by being there the Americans were invading New Brunswick's land. They must leave—or else. Instead of leaving, the Maine commander promptly arrested McLauchlin. As if to prove a higher degree of civility, the prisoner was taken by coach to Bangor and given the best accommodations available in the Bangor House.

Governor Fairfield delivered the "Message of the

Governor on the Invasion of Our Territory" to the legislature on February 18. He reported Lieutenant Governor Harvey's intention to send "a sufficient military force" to "repel what he thus regards as an Invasion of the Province of New Brunswick." Fairfield called for 1,500 men to rendezvous in Bangor and proceed to Aroostook's defense at the "earliest possible moment." He said Maine would call on the "President of the United States for aid in repelling the invasion of our territory by foreign troops" after he had a reply from New Brunswick regarding the return of McIntire *and* the removal of British-Canadian troops.

The Maine legislature was outraged by McIntire's arrest and the British-Canadian threats. Declaring the "honor and interest of this state" demanded action, they raised the stakes. The legislature called for a 10,000-man militia to defend Maine's northern territories, authorizing $800,000 and declaring war on New Brunswick.

A call to arms had been issued. The Dexter Artillery and Rifle Corps, Augusta Light Infantry, and militias from all over Maine eagerly rose to the challenge. Towns such as Waldo, Brewer, and Piscataquis sent volunteers heading for Bangor. The city's iron foundry quickly converted to casting musket balls.

Rufus McIntire was released "on parole" on February 21 (followed by McLauchlin), but the opposing troops stayed in place. Lieutenant Governor Harvey again demanded the Maine militia leave the disputed territory, promising he would send a force of British troops "in event of this request not being immediately complied with." Rumors abounded. Up to 5,000 British troops, including 1,000 Mohawk natives, were reported to be on their way to attack. Masardis asked for more reinforcements and prepared for the coming battle.

A mix of rumor, election year politics, and patriotism fueled war fever. The *Bangor Whig* announced: "Our state has been for the third time invaded and our citizens forcibly arrested, carried away, and incarcerated in a foreign jail." On February 26, Governor Fairfield addressed the soldiers gathering in Augusta before they headed for Aroostook. "An unfounded, unjust, and insulting claim of title has been made by the British government to more than one-third of the whole territory of your state."

Fearing imminent attack from New Brunswick, Maine asked President Martin Van Buren for backup. News mixed with rumors of bloodshed, and in March Congress authorized an effort to defend Maine's land claims. They ordered 50,000 federal troops to Aroostook and appropriated $10 million for the expedition. General Winfield Scott was appointed to take charge of the war zone, but Congress also urged a peaceful settlement if at all possible.

Fortunately for everyone, General Scott brought a cooler and calmer diplomacy. He was able to negotiate an agreement that neither side would proceed by force but would attempt one more diplomatic effort to settle the dispute. It worked. By May all the troops had returned home, their enlistment only lasting twenty-one to eighty-five days. The "war" was over. The closest thing to a battle was the fracas in the tavern the night McIntire was captured. Not a single shot was fired.

In 1842 the Webster–Ashburton Treaty, negotiated by Daniel Webster, finally settled the northern boundary of Maine: 5,012 square miles went to Great Britain, giving the British military overland access to Montreal; 7,015 square miles went to the United States. Great Britain paid Maine and Massachusetts $150,000 each, and the United States government promised to reimburse both states for their costs in defending the disputed area.

Maine remains the only state to have declared war on a foreign country. Despite the lack of ferocious battles or massive casualties, the message sent by the "Aroostook War" was clear. States took their borders seriously, and our national government was prepared to go to war to defend the borders of even a single state.

NOTE: Borders between states can also be disputed. Maine's southern border with New Hampshire (where Kittery, Maine, and Portsmouth, New Hampshire, meet) is still controversial. At the center of the dispute is a very profitable shipyard (along with over $5 million in Maine income tax from the New Hampshire residents working at the yard). Although named the Portsmouth Naval Shipyard, it is actually in Kittery. The 1740 decree of King George II set the boundary at the "middle of the river," placing the shipyard in Maine. New Hampshire argues that other evidence sets the border along the Maine shoreline, putting the shipyard in New Hampshire. The dispute went before the United States Supreme Court in 1976, resulting in a ruling for the "middle of the river" line. New Hampshire asked the court to reconsider in 2001, but the court stood by its earlier decision. While New Hampshire still disagrees, Maine considers the matter settled and there are no plans for a declaration of war over *this* border.

Race through
the Snow:
John Poor's Ride
to Win a Railway
· 1845 ·

John Poor watched the building clouds. The February weather had been clear and bright, but now the skies over Portland, Maine, were darkening. Concerned by the increasing winds and the beginnings of snow, thirty-seven-year-old Poor began packing. He quickly filled his satchel with maps, documents, and statistics that showed Portland to be the ideal southern end for a railway linking Canada and the United States. Montreal needed an ice-free winter port to use during the five months the Saint Lawrence River froze each year. Its Board of Trade was expected to choose Boston. Poor hoped to persuade them to consider Portland's advantages, but the vote was scheduled for February 10, just five days away. If Poor waited until the approaching storm passed, he would never reach Montreal in time. He had to try to beat the storm.

By 10:00 P.M. there were gale-force winds, and by midnight icy snow pellets clattered against the windows. Convinced it was "a turning point in the history of our railway," Poor strapped the satchel to his back and wrapped himself in furs. Climbing into a one-horse sleigh, he began the 300-mile journey.

Traveling all night, Poor had managed only 7 miles by 6:00 A.M. Over a foot of snow had fallen, and his horse was constantly dodging drifts. He switched his horse at Teak's Tavern in Falmouth, the first of several brief stops for fresh horses along the route. By noon eighteen inches covered the road, and the drifts were getting higher. Time after time, the sleigh overturned. Time after time, Poor righted the sleigh and climbed back in. His hands and feet became numb. The wind forced the snow horizontally; ice needles drove into Poor's skin and eyes.

Long after nightfall Poor arrived at his friend G. G. Waterhouse's South Paris home. Forty-seven miles down, over 250 to go, and he had been traveling almost twenty-four hours straight. The winds had shifted to the northwest, and now drifts were well over fence tops. Waterhouse convinced Poor to sleep for a few hours, planning to accompany him for the rest of the journey. At first light they headed for Andover with two horses and the single sleigh.

A half-dozen young men on their best horses were sent ahead of the sleigh to break a path through the deepening drifts. The temperature was eighteen degrees below zero when Poor's group reached Andover. The men took turns shoveling a trail for the horses and sleigh but averaged only 2 miles per hour. The deadline would be hard to meet if the storm continued. They all knew the most rugged terrain was still ahead.

At Dixville Notch the Bragg brothers of Erroll, New Hampshire, joined the group, as did a local guide called the Notch Tender, to assist in navigating the narrow passage between the 1,000-foot cliffs. Entering the pass, the men used shovels, making small footholds for the horses to follow. Men carried the sleigh and the baggage themselves. Then Poor saw "[a] huge mountain bank of snow piled at the bottom of the gorge, at the summit line of the road, perpendicular walls of snow to make one shudder at the mere recollection." A 20-foot snow drift, rising directly across the gorge, completely blocked the passage. Poor described "howling winds that roared and thundered like the bellows of the gods" as it seemed that nature had defeated them with this towering obstacle. But Poor refused to turn back. He, the Braggs, and three others shoveled for two more hours, opening a narrow cut through the enormous drift. The sky darkened with snow that continued to fall. As the men picked their way along the precarious path, they feared being smothered in an avalanche should the steep walls collapse in the wind. Committed to winning a rail connection to Canada, they pushed forward.

Poor had long advocated for a "national highway" of railroads. Bringing goods from all over the continent to the East Coast, it would open up trade throughout the world. If Portland became a coastal terminus, Maine could be a pivotal part of that potential trade. But to make that possible, Poor first had to get to Montreal.

After Dixville Notch the 18-inch snowfall on the other side seemed tame. Poor sent riders ahead to break the track and to engage more relay horses for the final push to Montreal.

At 5:30 A.M., on February 10, Poor's group arrived at the United States side of the Saint Lawrence River. After some searching they found a French-Canadian boatman willing to ferry them across the treacherous river in temperatures that hit twenty-nine degrees below zero. For over an hour they negotiated the dangerous waters, steering through broken and drifting ice floes. Finally, Poor arrived at his Montreal hotel at 7:00 A.M., having traveled 300 miles through the worst storm on record to that date. He had just three hours before the crucial meeting of the Montreal Board of Trade.

With only seven hours of sleep since leaving Portland five days before, Poor headed toward the ten o'clock meeting he had taken such risks to attend. After his courageous trip, Poor had a chance, and the element of surprise, but he had one more battle to win.

At 6 feet 2 inches, 250 pounds, John Poor was always an imposing figure and known to be a powerful speaker. Despite exhaustion and frostbite, Poor managed an eloquence that morning matched only by his meticulous preparation. He presented document after document; he described the natural depth and quality of Portland's harbor; he unrolled maps showing a possible 287-mile rail route (versus a 351-mile route from Boston) and demonstrating Portland's proximity to Europe (61 miles closer to Liverpool, England); he quoted detailed statistics on everything from shipping to crop prices. Hour after hour, Poor used his persuasive powers to itemize the advantages Portland offered. It worked! The board voted to delay the Boston resolution and consider Portland.

Debate continued for several days. On February 15th Judge William Pitt Preble arrived with the Maine legislature's official charter for the proposed Atlantic and Saint Lawrence Railway between Portland and Montreal, signed by Governor Hugh Anderson. On March 8 the Montreal Board of Trade finally agreed, voting in favor of the railway to Portland, and the Canadian legislature formally passed their charter for a rail line from Montreal to Portland just six days later.

Poor and Preble returned on March 20 to Portland, where a huge crowd of excited citizens gave the men a heroes' welcome with "loud and long continued cheering" before listening eagerly to details of the railway plan. Over the next few days, John Poor became ill, claiming only a "cold and a sore face from riding in the wind" in a letter to his brother Henry. Actually, Poor was weakened by pneumonia and still suffering from frostbite. When he collapsed weeks later, Poor's physician, Dr. George Shattuck, diagnosed "severe inflammation of the throat and lungs, extending to the Brain and through the alimentary canal—a Malignant influenza." Close to death for days, Poor slowly regained strength but continued to need crutches for months afterward. Twenty years later, Poor spoke of the lingering effects of his wild ride to Montreal:

> I could not go through such another exposure again, if I would, and I would not do it for all the wealth of the world.
>
> A snow-storm among the mountains is the most fearful thing in nature. The earthquake, the volcano, the hurricane are fearful exhibitions of the strife of the elements; but these, in the nature of things, are limited in extent and of short duration. But a snow-storm among the mountains or in the polar regions is a fearful type of vengeance, of terror, and of wrath. The dwellers in the city, or those who traverse the deep have no power to conceive of the sublimity or the grandeur of the snow-tempest among the hills. I made the trial once and found it more than my fancy had painted it. The recollection of it has haunted the writer of this as a lurid dream or a tormenting nightmare ever since.

Despite a population of only 16,000, Portland used local loans and stock subscriptions to raise over $3 million, and the railway was built. John Poor's trip may have been a "tormenting nightmare," but that incredible ride made it possible for his dream to become the reality known as the Grand Trunk Railway. The first 11 miles opened in 1848, and the entire route was completed by 1853, the first rail link between the United States and Canada. Poor founded the Portland Company Works in 1846, and the company eventually built more than 600 trains and over one hundred railway lines connecting the Northeast and Canada.

Over 150 years later, rail travel is no longer the dominant means of transportation, yet Poor's vision of national highways has come true. He always believed that Portland was "the natural seaport of Canada and the West." Through preparation, determination, and physical courage, John Poor enabled Portland to play a pivotal role in the development of railway trade, ensuring years of growth and economic gains for his beloved state of Maine.

The Start of a Habit
·1848·

John Curtis took a jackknife and scraped out a strip of the amber resin oozing from the cut in the felled spruce tree. Painstakingly, he shaped it into a somewhat round ball. The local Penobscots had been chewing spruce resin for years, but Curtis preferred it cooked, the way his father made it, so he tucked the ball into a cloth bag to take home when he was through working.

Born in Bradford, Maine, John Bacon Curtis spent most of his boyhood in nearby Hampden. He worked as a "swamper," starting at $5.00 a month, roughing out roads through the woods. While clearing trees and underbrush for the new roads, he often noticed the sap on fallen spruce. His father had sometimes pulled the strips of resin off, brought them home, and made them into chewable chunks for himself and friends. Now nineteen, Curtis had little schooling, but he had an idea. Why not start a business making the spruce resin into chewing gum and selling it?

In the 1840s gum chewing was highly unusual and was certainly not socially acceptable. Lumbermen had picked up the habit from natives and had occasionally gathered and sold resin to earn extra cash. Curtis dreamed of shipping and selling gum all around the country. Two years later, he and his father began a business.

First they collected quantities of spruce resin. Curtis hired farm boys and out-of-work lumbermen to go into the woods for a day or two at a time to gather the sap. Spruce sap is normally released by trees that have been struck by lightning, split by frost, or injured by woodpeckers or squirrels. The sap is nature's way of protecting exposed wood, allowing the tree to heal. Spruce sap is also released as a result of lumbering, both from cut spruce trees and those scraped by falling trees. Scraping the resin from the trees was painstaking work and bits of bark, twigs, and leaves were often mixed in with the sap.

Once the sap resin was gathered, the rest of the process was done in the Curtis's kitchen. The resin was thrown, twigs, bark, and all, into a big black kettle and boiled on their Franklin stove. After cooking to the consistency of molasses, it was strained to skim off the bark and twigs, leaving just the cooked resin. To cool, it was poured onto a slab and rolled until about ¼-inch thick. To market, it was cut into ½-inch-wide strips, then into ¾-inch pieces. The entire batch was dusted with cornstarch so that, when packed into small wooden boxes, it wouldn't stick to the packing paper layers.

When the first batch was ready to be marketed, the price of gum was two for a penny and packaged twenty pieces to a box. Curtis went door-to-door in Portland looking for merchants to sell the new "State of Maine Pure Spruce Gum." The first willing merchant quickly sold out of his first order and a business was born. The first to manufacture chewing gum commercially, Curtis & Son made over $5,000 in the first year, a huge success in 1848.

Spruce gum was definitely an acquired taste, more prized for its texture than its flavor. When you first put a nugget of golden brown spruce gum in your mouth, it has the consistency of a small rock. Then it breaks into smaller pieces that congeal into a mixture that bears more resemblance to cement than to today's chewing gum, putting teeth and dentures at risk. However, unlike today's gum, spruce gum could be chewed for hours before the flavor, slightly bitter as it was, faded.

The taste may have been bitter, but soon it seemed everyone was chewing spruce gum. Curtis peddled the gum to a growing base of merchants, and soon the company outgrew the family kitchen. The Curtises moved to nearby Bangor and found a 15-by-15-foot square space for the business. They bought gum resin by the pound from pickers who went to the woods for as little as a day or two at a time. Still using a single stove, the elder Curtis was in charge of supervising the manufacture, while his son continued to market the gum.

As Curtis & Son grew, they moved the business to 231 Congress Street in Portland, where they had multiple stoves and over a dozen employees. After the 1866 Portland fire, they built a three-story brick building on the corner of Fore and Deer Streets, the first in the world exclusively for the manufacture and packaging of chewing gum.

Needing large quantities of spruce resin, Curtis employed groups of pickers to go into the woods for weeks at a time, working furiously during the few short months of the sap season. Going in, they brought a sled loaded with wooden barrels full of extra clothes, dry beans, salt pork, flour, tin dishes, and tobacco. Pickers often followed woodsmen, chopping the resin off downed trees with an ax. To gather sap from tall standing spruce, they developed a special tool, described in the *Portland Board of Trade Journal:*

> It consists of a long pole, upon the top of which is a little sack that will hold about two quarts of gum. Back of this sack is a piece of iron or steel made like a hammer and working upon a pivot, while a cord is attached to the end and extends to the foot of the pole. The picker places the top of this picking machine along the gummy seam of the spruce, and by operating the little hammer, by means of the cord, is able to clip off the lumps of gum into the sack, located under the top of the hammer.

If the tree had a particularly well-filled seam, a picker might get several quarts, but a more typical tree would yield a pint of resin. Most was an amber color, but prize resin was clear, almost bright. Pickers would put the collected resin into the now-empty barrels and load them onto the sled to be carried for miles out of the woods.

John Curtis earned respect for his fairness and hard work. His slogan was, "Give a man all you can for his money, while making a fair profit yourself." He paid attention to the details. The wooden display boxes were handmade and sometimes elaborately carved with flowers and trees. The first few years, he peddled the gum personally all over New England. He placed advertisements in local papers, gaining business for merchants who carried his gum.

A shrewd businessman, Curtis also recognized the importance of putting profits into improving the business. At one point he took $50 out of the profits and used it to experiment with and develop more efficient machinery for the factory. Although his father thought it a waste of time and money, Curtis proved him wrong. Despite having had little schooling, he invented machines that enabled workers to go from hand packing forty boxes a day to turning out 1,800 boxes of gum daily at their peak. With an average output of 1,000 boxes per day, the workforce grew to almost 200 employees, mostly women.

Curtis advertised his gum as "Preparations of superior SPRUCE CHEWING GUM Neatly put up in boxes," and soon shipped gum across Canada and as far as Honolulu and Mexico City. In probably the largest ever raw spruce sale, the company once paid $35,000 for roughly ten tons. By 1899 a news article said Curtis & Son "enjoyed a monopoly in the chewing gum business in the United States and, in fact, in the world."

Chewing spruce gum quickly became a national habit. Adults chewed it, often as a substitute for tobacco, and children couldn't get enough of it. In Mark Twain's *Tom Sawyer,* Becky

Thatcher gives spruce gum to Tom and finding it agreeable, "they chewed it turn about, and dangled their legs against the bench in excess of contentment." Its prized status among children was demonstrated in Twain's *Huckleberry Finn,* when Tom tells Huck about the powers of magic genies to "build a palace forty miles long out of Di'monds, and fill it full of chewing gum." It sold for a penny a stick, and it was purchased by everyone from children in small towns to presidents in the White House. Robert Frost even wrote about spruce gum's mystique in his 1916 poem "The Gum-Gatherer":

> What this man brought in a cotton sack
> Was gum, the gum of the mountain spruce.
> He showed me lumps of the scented stuff
> Like uncut jewels, dull and rough.
> It comes to market golden brown,
> But turns to pink between the teeth.

Gum gatherers were often hired by middlemen, who would provide them with food and clothes, find a market for the gum, and split the profits with the crew. But Curtis hired his own crews from the beginning, and these skilled gum pickers often gathered 4,000 pounds in a single season.

After the turn of the century, however, spruce gum had competition. Other more tasty varieties of gum began to enter the market. Curtis developed a sweetened paraffin-based gum and added it to their line. But the biggest blow came when a competitor developed a chicle-based gum. It quickly gained popularity over the less-flavorful spruce gum.

The spruce gum harvest, which averaged more than 150 tons annually at the turn of the century, slipped to barely 5 tons by 1932. The dozen competing Maine gum manufacturers dwindled until the last one, the Kennebec Spruce Gum Company, faded into oblivion in the 1970s. The sweetened paraffin gum Curtis developed still can be found in fake lips, mustaches, and fangs at Halloween or in joke stores, but chicle-based gums have replaced the bitter taste of spruce gum.

Americans chew billions of sticks of gum each year, and the United States now exports almost a million kilograms of chewing gum worth an estimated $3.5 billion annually. Children of all ages are indebted to a man whose name they've never heard. They share a national habit that started with a Maine father and son boiling tree sap on their kitchen stove.

The Vision That Began a War
·1851·

The winter of 1850 was Maine's coldest in years, and Harriet Beecher Stowe struggled to keep her family warm. Calvin Stowe was a religion professor at Brunswick's Bowdoin College, but he had gone back to Ohio to finish up some business. Harriet was left with the full responsibility of maintaining the house and managing their children. Pregnant with their seventh child, she had arrived in Brunswick the previous summer and had gotten the family settled. Their home was drafty at best, and by winter it became almost impossible to keep warm. Pails of water turned to ice, and sometimes biscuit dough actually froze to the board before it could be rolled out.

Deeply religious, Harriet was troubled by the practice of slavery. Her family was full of ministers, and like most religious white families in the North, they were vehemently opposed to slavery. In private, they supported the Underground Railroad. In public, they preached fiery sermons against slavery from their pulpits. Her relatives encouraged Harriet to write a story against slavery. She had supplemented the family income in Ohio by writing for newspapers and local magazines, but she had been too busy to write since moving to Maine. The idea appealed to Stowe, but she doubted she would ever find the time.

The Stowes attended church regularly at First Parish Church on Route One, across from the Bowdoin College campus. On March 2, 1851, Harriet and the children trudged through the snow for Sunday morning worship and settled into the straight-backed, narrow seat of pew twenty-three.

As the morning's service began, Harriet looked forward to communion. She'd always been moved by its familiar peace and comfort. The scripture that day was from the book of Revelation, though at the time no one knew what a coincidence that would turn out to be. From the pulpit towering more than 7 feet above the congregation, the Reverend George E. Adams began his sermon. Light shone through the clear glass windows, with occasional accents of color from the narrow strip of colored glass that framed each window.

Suddenly, the church seemed alive with bright colors, radiating an almost heavenly light. The other parishioners seemed to fade away as a totally different scene formed in front of Harriet. She later described seeing "an old Negro, dying after having been lashed by a slave overseer, while a lovely child looked down from heaven." The vision was so realistic that Stowe was shaken by its violence. Tears came to her eyes as she watched the scene unfold in her mind.

Stowe saw two black men torturing and beating another black man. The old man was bleeding as he was whipped to the point of death. A white man looked on, filled with hatred, encouraging the cruelty. As the old man fell to the ground and neared death, he looked up at the men torturing him and forgave them. He went to glory in Heaven, having escaped his enemies in death and having conquered them with his forgiveness, even as the whipping took his life.

Shaken by her vision, Stowe gathered her children and rushed out of the church. Hurrying the 2 blocks down Cleveland Street and over to their Federal Street home, Stowe immediately went to her room and began writing at a small gateleg table. When Stowe lived in Ohio, she had heard stories of such violence from runaway slaves hidden in her family's home. The fugitives had described cruel overseers, the terror of fleeing in the night to avoid slave hunters, and families ripped apart, separated at the auction block or sold to different owners. Moving to Maine, she had expected the slavery issue to seem more distant. Writing feverishly to capture her vision on paper, she saw the horrors of slavery once again, very personal and very real.

The children played and read as Stowe filled page after page, capturing the details of her vision. When she ran out of paper, she asked the children to bring her brown wrapping paper scraps to use. Finished, she read it to her older children. Hearing the vivid brutality to the old slave, they burst into tears and urged their mother to publish it so that everyone would know slavery's horror. But Stowe put the pages in a drawer. The story was terribly brutal and violent. The scene was incomplete. Why was the slave she named "Tom" being beaten? Who was the sweet child looking down from Heaven? Stowe had a scene, but not a book.

Having put the pages aside, Harriet went back to her daily tasks. But the story was not so easily banished. Images continued coming to her mind, scene after scene, built on memories from Ohio. Her initial vision had been of one old slave, escaping through death. As the weeks passed, her mind filled with fragments of characters and events. Stowe knew that to portray the institution of slavery, she needed a thread or a framework to bring the stories together.

Later that March, Calvin came home, found the pages in the drawer, and sat down to read. Deeply moved, he encouraged Harriet to finish. Combining the new images and characters with those of her vision, she began. She wrote Dr. Gamaliel Bailey, an abolitionist editor she knew, and proposed a story:

> My object will be to hold up in the most lifelike and graphic manner possible, Slavery, its reverses, changes, and the negro character, which I have had

ample opportunities for studying . . . . The thing may extend through three or four numbers. It will be ready in two or three weeks.

Dr. Bailey agreed, offering $300. Harriet began, and in June 1851, the first installment of *Uncle Tom's Cabin* was published in *National Era,* Bailey's Washington, D.C.–based newspaper. Readers were touched by the plight of the characters and were shocked by the horror of Stowe's vivid images. Writing in snatches at home and at her husband's office in Appleton Hall, Stowe wrote episode after episode. More than a year later, Stowe brought the story to a close. The "three or four installments" had turned out to be over forty. Stowe's original Sunday morning vision became a pivotal chapter titled "The Martyr."

When *Uncle Tom's Cabin* was published as a complete two-volume book in 1852, it broke all records. The initial print run was 5,000 copies. The first day 3,000 were sold, and the remaining sold the next day. In the United States alone, first-year sales topped 300,000 copies. Despite having three mills supplying paper for the book and eight power printing presses running twenty-four hours a day, the publisher's supply ran thousands of copies behind orders.

The Stowes moved to Andover, Massachusetts, not long after *Uncle Tom's Cabin* was published. In 1862 Harriet and two of her children traveled to Washington, D.C., to meet President Abraham Lincoln. It is widely reported that on meeting her, Lincoln remarked, "So you're the little woman who wrote the book that made this great war." Whether the remark is fact or folklore, *Uncle Tom's Cabin* neither caused the war nor helped settle the slavery debate peacefully, as she had hoped.

Stowe remained humble and self-effacing, asserting God had authored *Uncle Tom's Cabin,* saying, "The Lord Himself wrote it. I was but an instrument in his hand." Shortly after the success of *Uncle Tom's Cabin,* Harriet described herself as "a little bit of a woman, somewhat more than forty, about as thin and dry as a pinch of snuff, never very much to look at in my best days, and looking like a used up article now." Stowe was hardly used up. She continued to write, averaging a book a year for more than twenty years, although nothing else she wrote came close to her earliest success. Before coming to Brunswick, she was asked by a publisher for a brief biographical sketch. She replied: "[H]aving reflected duly and truly on my past life, it is so uneventful and uninteresting that I do not see how anything can be done for me in the way of a sketch . . . the greater portion of my time and strength has been spent in the necessary but unpoetic duties of the family."

Perhaps Stowe's life had seemed uneventful then, but not after one cold Maine Sunday. The impact of her vision changed Stowe's life. Her book was published in dozens of languages and has been changing lives around the world for over 150 years. Since the first installment appeared in 1851, *Uncle Tom's Cabin* has never been out of print.

Lighthouse Teen
·1856·

Matinicus Rock is a barren granite outcropping beyond the entrance to Penobscot Bay well off Matinicus Island. The original lighthouse station was built in 1827, a combination of twin wooden light towers and dwellings for the keeper's family. The wood towers were replaced by sturdier stone towers in 1848. Five years later, Captain Samuel Burgess became the lightkeeper and moved to the rocky outpost with his sickly wife and the four youngest of his children.

Tending a lighthouse was a challenging and extremely labor-intensive task. The days of automated electric lights were still a hundred years in the future. Light was provided by the flame of oil lamps set in front of reflector pans. The lamps had to be kept burning from sunset to sunrise daily and whenever fog or clouds reduced daytime visibility. There could be no chance that even a single lamp would go out during the night, so keepers had to stay up all night, every night. There were no sick days. There were no days off.

Family members pitched in with the daily upkeep. In addition to the typical winding staircase with hundreds of steps, light towers included windows, passageways, and rooms for oil, equipment, and supplies. The young children helped by sweeping the landings, stairs, and storage rooms. The oldest, fourteen-year-old Abbie, learned how to care for the oil lamps. Soon she was able to trim their hollow wicks and clean the reflective lenses as well as her father could.

The Burgesses relied on supply boats that came twice a year to restock food, oil, and other necessities. In January 1856, they were still waiting for the September boat. They had enough oil and food for the moment, but not enough to last until the spring boat. And Burgess's wife needed more medicine. The nearest real town was Rockland, 25 miles away. With no other choice, Captain Burgess left Abbie and the family and set off. A storm came up almost immediately after he sailed. Without modern weather forecasting, it was impossible to know when he would be able to return. In the meantime Abbie was on her own and in charge.

Abbie went about her work. There was a total of twenty-eight lamps in the two towers. Each lamp's dustpan reflectors had to be cleaned of soot daily. The slightest film of soot would prevent them from reflecting maximum light. Each day the hollow wick of every lamp had to be kept trimmed perfectly to give off peak light. The thick strain of whale oil used for the lamps in summer had already been switched for a thinner whale oil. But in the extreme cold, even the thinner oil congealed. Each time the lamps needed refilling, Abbie had to heat the oil before carrying it to the lanterns. Days turned into a week. Abbie knew how to do all this, but she also knew the terrible consequences if the lights were to dim or go out for even just a short time. The responsibility was huge. One week turned into two.

On January 19 the continuing storm became so severe that the winds literally shook the wooden keeper's quarters. The storm surge, combined with high tides, threatened to flood the entire outpost. Because of her mother's illness, Abbie was also responsible for the family. Worried for their safety, Abbie moved everyone out of the unstable building and into one of the newer, sturdier light towers built on the high ground. It proved to be a choice that saved their lives. In a long letter to a friend on the mainland, Abbie later described the events of the seemingly endless storm:

[T]he windows [shutters] had to be secured to prevent the violence of the spray from breaking them in. As the tide came, the sea rose higher and higher, till the only endurable places were the lighttowers. If they stood we were saved, otherwise our fate was only too certain.

The Burgess family had a coop full of hens they raised for eggs and as companions. Despite her mother's warnings to stay inside, Abbie was determined to save their hens from the storm. Abbie's account continued:

Seizing a basket, I ran out a few yards after the rollers had passed and the sea fell off a little, with the water knee deep, to the coop, and rescued all but one. It was the work of a moment, and I was back . . . the door fastened, but none too quick, for at that instant my little sister, standing at a window, exclaimed, "Oh look! look there! the worst sea is coming!"

Abbie had made it to safety just in time. Looking out the window, Abbie watched as not only the coop, but their old quarters washed away. In the letter Abbie told what happened, "[T]he sea made a complete breach over the rock, washing every movable thing away, and of the old dwelling not one stone was left upon another of the foundation."

Abbie continued tending the lights and watching over her family as the storm raged. The windows in the gallery around the lights became coated with ice. They needed to be cleared constantly despite the danger as sheets of salt spray were blown across the rocks. Sleet and snow severely limited visibility. Abbie described the noise of the storm: "The sea is never still, and when agitated, its roar shuts out every other sound, even drowning our voices." Day and night ran together in a blur of impossible fatigue, cold, and noise. Abbie kept going. Gradually, the storm began to subside. Nearly four weeks passed before the sea was finally calm enough for Abbie's father to return. During the entire time the Matinicus lights remained steady. Abbie did not realize what a remarkable accomplishment that was. As she wrote her friend:

> For some reason, I know not why, I had no misgivings and went on with my work as usual . . . Though at times greatly exhausted by my labors, not once did the lights fail. Under God I was able to perform all my accustomed duties as well as my father's.

Four years later, when Captain John Grant was appointed lightkeeper, Abbie stayed on to train him in the idiosyncrasies of the Matinicus Rock Light Station. Grant's son, Isaac, was going to be the assistant lightkeeper, so he needed to learn the ropes also. They worked together for months, and within a year Isaac and Abbie were married. They stayed and Isaac took over as lightkeeper. Abbie raised four children on Matinicus Rock, serving as a salaried "lighthouse assistant" before being transferred to White Head Light in 1872 and promoted to "keeper." She and Isaac continued as lightkeepers until ill health forced their retirement in 1890. Abbie missed her lights terribly and died fewer than two years later. She tried to explain her relationship with the lights in a letter written shortly before her death:

> Sometimes I think the time is not far distant when I shall climb these lighthouse stairs no more. It has always seemed to me that the light was part of myself . . . In all these years I always put the lamps in order in the morning and I lit them at night. These old lamps on Matinicus Rock . . . I often dream of them.

When I dream of them it always seems to me that I have been away a long while, and I am hurrying toward the Rock to light the lamps there before sunset.

One of the best known women lightkeepers, Abbie has had her story made into several children's books and even a musical. Her fame began with her actions as a teen, but her legacy is built on a lifetime of service. From the age of fourteen, Abbie spent her life in isolated lighthouses. She never considered herself extraordinary. Through storm and calm, a Maine lightkeeper's job was to protect the safety of seagoing people and vessels. Abbie was a lightkeeper.

Desolation!
Desolation!
· 1866 ·

Captain G. M. Dinsmore ordered the sails taken in as the schooner *Clara* approached Jonesport Harbor. Two men climbed the rigging, surefooted despite the 11:00 P.M. blackness. Looking to the south, they immediately knew something was terribly wrong. They saw an unnatural red glow just along the horizon. Not until the next day did they learn the glow was a fire 200 miles to the south, destroying the heart of Maine's largest city.

For days the *Portland Transcript* and other newspapers had touted festivities for the first Fourth of July celebrations since Maine's 4,000 Civil War veterans had returned. Every hotel and boarding home in Portland was full. John Wood's magnificent new six-story Marble Hotel was finished but not quite ready to open. Bailey & Company's Circus advertised "that greatest marvel of the Animal Kingdom and Antediluvian wonder, the gigantic HIPPOPOTAMUS! . . . the Behemoth of Holy Writ." After the parade, "Messrs. Sever & Starkweler of Boston" would provide hot air balloon rides beginning at noon. The committee announced band concerts and "for splendor and extent, this display of Fire-Works [that] will eclipse any ever before exhibited east of Boston."

The celebrations began with the ringing of bells for an hour at sunrise and again at noon. The promised sunset bells never rang, because in midafternoon a small fire began in a waterfront boat shop near Brown's Sugar House. The Sugar House was a huge eight-story plant covering nearly an acre of waterfront, employing 1,000, and granulating 250 barrels of sugar daily. With walls made of four brick layers, it seemed fire-proof.

The fire began unnoticed, as most people were off celebrating in the city center. The boat shop was a mass of flames already spreading to a pile of boards before the first firefighters arrived. The flames moved to a planing shop whose carpentry fueled the fire. The planing shop and adjacent machine shop were quickly engulfed. Then nature conspired to assist the fire. Just as the Cotton Street cistern's water ran out, the wind sprang up from the southwest, carrying exploding sparks to nearby buildings and beyond. Soon the one-hundred-gallon molasses casks outside the Sugar House were on fire and the great building began to burn. The wind grew stronger, fanning the flames.

Firemen were ill-equipped for the wind-driven shower of sparks as the fire grew. Portland had no pressure-fed running water, just cellar cisterns for rainwater and town pumps scattered around the city. The single leather scuttle pails hanging from nails at each public pump, combined with home scuttles, were the city's first line of defense, designed to fight small house fires. Hose wagons had dozens more for use in bucket brigades until pumping engines could arrive, but no bucket brigade could stop a fire this size.

The summer had been dry, and reservoirs contained only a few hundred gallons of water. Even the ocean had literally turned against them. As pumps emptied the wells and cisterns, men stretched their hoses to the wharves to use salt water. But the tide was nearly at its lowest point and would be of little help fighting the growing conflagration.

People soon noticed the smoke overhead and turned to see the glow from the waterfront as bells finally rang out over the city sounding the alarm. The bell of Saint Stephen's church kept ringing, even as flames began to consume the building. As the smoke deepened, and the glow became a line of flames, people began to gather their belongings. But which way would the wind take the fire? Where was safety?

The fire burned a diagonal line across the city, and soon danger seemed everywhere. Large pieces of flaming shingles flew airborne the length of the city, igniting houses almost a mile from the original fire. Some tried to protect their roofs with water-soaked quilts but soon fled, defeated.

Children carted belongings for neighbors and strangers. A baseball club worked putting out the burning cinders as they fell on a roof, saving one home a bit beyond the edge of the fire. Some, unable to transport their things to safety, hurriedly dug a trench and buried them, hoping to to dig up the valuables from the ashes when the flames had passed.

One shop owner near the fire's edge used water, then barrels of beef pickle brine, to douse the flaming embers as they dropped on his business. He was down to only two remaining buckets of vinegar when the fire finally moved past. (Newspapers later found small humor describing "the brick wall on which the salt became encrusted is surely in a pretty *pickle*.")

In the rush for safety, the bizarre went barely noticed. Dwarfs and circus clowns, still made up for the performance, helped homeowners load belongings into the garishly painted circus wagons that were pressed into service. Zebras were hooked to pull carriages full of people and possessions away from the fire's path. The fire's noise drowned out the tinkling of the silver bells that were tied into the manes of circus horses as their drivers made trip after trip, carrying people from danger. Trainer Charles Johnson even pressed his elephants, Anthony, Cleopatra, Victoria, and Albert, into service. When the fire reached Charles Day's warehouse, the holiday fireworks and rockets were set off, their explosions mixing with the sound of collapsing walls.

People abandoned their homes as the air became thick with burning wood embers. Falling cinders burned large holes in their clothes, and people burned their hands extinguishing the flames. John Neal later described the horror:

> [A] great roaring was heard afar off, and coming nearer and nearer the doorsteps and housetops . . . The heavens gathered blackness and a hurricane of fire swept over the city, carrying cinders and blazing fragments of wood far into the country . . . On swept the whirlwind of fire, spreading out like a fan as it went, directly through the wealthiest and busiest part of our city.

Firemen never had a chance against the fierce wind driving the fire inexorably through the city center, but they never gave up. Fire companies telegraphed of the disaster converged on Portland from Lewiston, Saco, and Biddeford. As the fight continued into the night, firemen arrived from Boston, 100 miles away, to assist the exhausted Portland firemen, who continued to fight despite singed hair, blistered hands, and scorched faces.

They tried everything to stop the destruction. One fireman drove an open carriage loaded with kegs of explosives while holding a blanket over them to protect the explosives from flying embers and sparks. The explosives were to bring down buildings to create a firebreak. Others pulled wooden buildings down with ropes, but nothing stopped the fire. One curious man timed the burning of Captain Tolford's Congress Street home, and from the first visible flame until it was completely leveled took just seven minutes. The flames swept over John Wood's magnificent hotel, burning it to the ground before it ever welcomed a guest. City Hall burned to a hollow shell. Street by street, the fire's path stretched, forming a mile of flames at its widest point. Finally, the fire reached the sand piles and pig pastures on Munjoy Hill and ran out of fuel to burn. Like a child whose temper is spent, the fire quieted and, at last, was still.

In fifteen hours one-third of Portland had been leveled. The fire destroyed 1,500 homes, 8 churches, 8 hotels, 4 schools, and 3 public and countless private libraries. Roughly one hundred manufacturing plants, almost all of the retail businesses (including all nine banks, all seven printing houses, every law office and newspaper), the historical society, custom house, and city hall were also reduced to ash. Devastating a swath of 58 streets, 320 acres of an active, thriving city had been decimated, an estimated loss of over $10 million.

Visiting Portland a few weeks after the fire, Henry Wadsworth Longfellow looked over the barren landscape. His own home was outside the fire's path, but just blocks away there was nothing but a scattering of blackened chimneys and charred tree trunks poking above the deep ashes. He wrote a friend: "Desolation! Desolation! Desolation! It reminds me of the ruins of Pompeii."

Reporters and photographers rushed to Portland. *Harper's Weekly* covered it with photos and text describing the most disastrous fire in United States history. Frank Leslie summed it up for the July 28 issue of New York's *Illustrated Newspaper:*

> It is a sad reflection that a simple spark of fire . . . caught up by the winds of heaven, should, in a single night, annihilate the labors of thousands of industrious and energetic men . . . What a few days ago was a beautiful, active, throbbing city is now a desolate waste, a scarred and scorched, and blackened monument of ruin.

Out of the Ashes
· 1866 ·

Early in the morning of July 5, 1866, Portland's leaders met at First Parish Church and started plans for immediate relief. Thousands of Portland's citizens were homeless and a third of the city had burned in the great fire that was finally dying out as their meeting began. By 10:00 A.M. a temporary outdoor kitchen was set up and serving anyone who needed food. By the second serving at 6:00 that night, relief workers were handing out blankets and clothes too. For weeks free meals were served at 10:00 A.M. and 6:00 P.M., giving strength and encouragement to those who had lost everything. The afternoon train from Boston brought $13,000 for relief and three carloads of cooked food. New York telegraphed that it had pledges of $100,000 for assistance.

Everywhere people shared their stories. Elizabeth Day was, at ninety-nine years, Portland's oldest resident. She had vivid memories of being a seven-year-old, in colonial Portland, watching British Captain Mowatt sail his fleet up the harbor and begin its bombardment. As much of the city burned, she remembered seeing her father's Fore Street house, where she had been born, go up in flames. Now she had watched as some of the homes that had escaped the 1775 fire succumbed to this fire. It was her son's fireworks that were set off prematurely by the blaze.

Hannah Thurlow, ninety-one, also survived both fires, though she had no memories of 1775. She had been carried from her India Street home to safety, an infant in the arms of her father. Now infirm, she had again been carried to safety from the rebuilt India Street home, this time by her grandchildren.

Fire Engineer Wiggins fought the fire at Cumberland and Franklin Streets until the heat broke the glass in Engine Number 8's ornamental lantern. Brushing sparks off the horses' backs, Wiggins moved to a safer point to fight.

The most astounding survival story was that of a man whose story is well documented, but whose name was never recorded. Arrested for public drunkenness, he had been placed in cell number 15 in the basement of the City Building. Passed out, he was overlooked when the other prisoners were released as the fire approached. He slept through the danger, oblivious to the inferno that burned above and around him. At 10:00 A.M. the morning after the fire, men clearing rubble heard his cries and dug him out of the ruined building. His cell was on the west side of the building, facing away from the high wind and fire. An open window allowed him air. He had survived virtually unharmed.

That afternoon the *Portland Transcript* published a broadsheet, printed in Lewiston and distributed in Portland. The account of the fire had been written the previous night as it still raged. But was it over? With emotion shown by large type and bold fonts, Mayor Stevens warned:

> citizens of Portland, who still have Dwellings or Stores standing, [of] the importance of keeping a strict **WATCH TO-NIGHT!** And also of having BUCKETS and TUBS of WATER at hand to keep their roofs well wet, as a change of the wind would re-kindle the fire and destroy the Western portion of the City.

But the fire did not return and Portlanders made a critical choice. With fierce determination they turned their back on their losses and chose to rebuild.

The cleanup began even as the burned ground was still

warm. Parishioners of Saint Stephen's found only misshapen blobs left of the bell that had fallen, broken, and melted as their church burned. Ashes were shoveled into barrels. Lumps of melted nails were scooped up to be reclaimed and reshaped. Practicality won over emotion as decisions were made. The post office, customhouse, and city hall were deemed irreparable, were demolished, and the land cleared for rebuilding. Most buildings were completely gone already, with only an occasional wall or chimney left at the edge of a cellar hole full of white ash.

City leaders encouraged Portlanders as in the July 6 editorial in the *Portland Evening Star:*

> It is almost too much for the mind to grasp . . . yet we can but counsel hopefulness and patience . . . to the brave and true all things are possible . . . We still have our wharves and harbor and land . . . We can still supply our own trade and keep that which we had growing in the East . . . [We] are manned by men who have brains and pluck. . . . in the presence of such calamity let us assert all the manhood [of] our united strength and though we may be cast down we cannot be disturbed.

That same edition carried a new directory of businesses, letting customers know the new, temporary locations of physicians, lawyers, music dealers, and hairdressers. Column after column listed businesses burned, their losses, and insurance coverage. Most were like Haines, Smith and Clark Hardware (loss $50,000, insurance $2,600) or Judge Clifford (library's loss $12,000, no insurance).

Miraculously, only two people died in the fire. First reports showed no fatalities, but four days after the fire, two bodies were found. An eleven-year-old invalid, Sabin Chickering, and his mother had been trapped on the fourth floor of a Washington

Street residence and were overcome by smoke as the lower floors burned, barring rescue or escape.

Assistance poured in to the city. Congress sent $50,000 and temporarily stopped collecting taxes. The secretary of war ordered 1,500 tents sent to shelter the homeless. Army troops prevented looting and guarded the banks now operating from hastily organized offices in cashiers' homes. Relief money came from Montreal and Saint John, Canada, and cities as far as Philadelphia, Chicago, and Cleveland, eventually totaling $600,000.

On July 16 Bailey & Company's Circus returned to Portland. People left the Munjoy Hill tent city and joined other residents in an impromptu parade. Everyone cheered the drivers and all those who had pitched in so selflessly to help during the fire.

By August the sounds of hammers and saws were everywhere. Homes and businesses taking shape began dotting the expanse, and by October one could no longer look across the fire's barren scar. The city seized the opportunity to make improvements as they rebuilt. Some of the 47 miles of burned streets were realigned or widened, and many small alleys were eliminated. The city raced the seasons to get as much rebuilt as possible before winter.

Mainers normally take winter in stride, slowing their pace only as weather requires, and following the ebb and flow of seasons as well as tides. But this winter there was no slowing, regardless of weather, as John Neal's January 27, 1867, journal attested:

> Within the last month . . . we have had two of the toughest and heaviest snowstorms I ever saw; and are now up to the waist in another . . . And yet, our people are swarming to their work, early and late; the city is going up silently through the deep snow, block after block, and street after street.

Portland did go back up, and on January 1, 1868, Neal wrote, "Another year! Portland is now rebuilt, and greatly enlarged and beautiful." Congress Street became the heart of the new business district, and the city acted quickly to avoid future fires. A 20-inch main brought water from Sebago Lake to Portland. A 12-million-gallon reservoir was built on Bramhall Hill, and by 1870 distribution pipes throughout the city were completed.

The fire has not been forgotten. As late as the 1940s, the outline of the fire's path could be seen in the spring from the air by noting the difference in tree planting and growth. Renovations to the wharf area and "new" customhouse in 1976 unearthed some unusual rubble. Tests showed it to be from the demolition of the original customhouse after the 1866 fire.

Anniversaries are still noted, and Portland papers still print special inserts recounting the statistics and retelling some of the stories. But as the years go on, the articles focus less on the devastation. Like the Portlanders of 1775 and 1866, today's residents choose to focus on the positive. Portland is still the largest city in Maine. A thriving center of business, Portland is alive with a multitude of activities for visitors and locals. The vibrant city is its own best monument, honoring the determination and vigor with which Portland again rose from ashes to even greater strength and beauty.

The Hunt for a Prize
·1897·

"Fly Rod" Crosby moved with a strength and athleticism honed over years in the Maine outdoors. As her nickname implied, Cornelia Crosby's fly-fishing prowess was legendary. She had hunted and fished all over the woods, rivers, and lakes of northern and western Maine. The first woman acknowledged to fish "regularly and systematically with a light fly rod and artificial bait of flies," she held a record on Maine's Kennebago Lake for catching 200 trout in one day. But today she was hunting the most prized member of the deer family, the caribou. Six feet tall and lithe, Crosby picked her way confidently through the woods around Aroostook County's Square Lake. Twenty-five years earlier, her doctor had worried that Crosby was suffering from tuberculosis. Today there was not a single, observable remnant of the young woman he had pronounced "soft of muscle, anemic and consumptive."

Crosby had taken the doctor's advice for "a large dose of outdoors." Discovering a passion for camping, hunting, and fishing, she wanted others to find that same passion. She described the beauty and joy of the Maine woods for readers all over the country in a series of articles called "Fly-Rod's Notebook." Appearing in magazines and newspapers in New York, Boston, Philadelphia, and Chicago, the column made Crosby a one-woman publicity campaign for the state she called "the Nation's Playground." But today she was not interested in bringing others to Maine. She was focused on the ground in front of each step, searching for any sign that a caribou had passed.

Though not plentiful, in 1897 caribou still roamed through Maine, a rare prize for any hunter. Crosby wanted to add a caribou to her collection of hunting trophies. The previous winter she had tramped mile after mile through deep snow with no success. For ten days she hunted in near zero temperatures, but when the weather worsened, Crosby was forced to give up and wait for another year. With renewed determination she was now at D. L. Cummings's camp for another try.

Given her experience in the Maine woods, some might have been surprised that Crosby used a guide. Cummings was well known for successful hunts around Square Lake, and Crosby knew the benefits of an expert guide familiar with the local area. The previous February she had spoken before the state legislature supporting legislation to evaluate and license qualified guides. On March 19 the bill passed, and to honor her role promoting Maine to people all over the country, the legislature officially awarded Maine guide license number one to Cornelia "Fly Rod" Crosby.

Crosby and Cummings headed to Square Lake, where caribou had been seen, and eagerly began the hunt. Both knew that if they actually saw any of the elusive game, they probably couldn't move close enough for a good shot before startling them off. Their best chance was to let the caribou come to them. Caribou root beneath the snow and eat just the freshest moss. Then they often retrace their route, cleaning up the older moss before moving to a new grazing area. Crosby inspected the snowy ground looking for a spot where the snow was scraped aside but some gray moss still showed. That would be the place to lie in wait. For three days Crosby and Cummings picked their way around the shore with no luck.

When fishing, Fly Rod generally wore a dark, long-sleeved, belted jacket and sporty hat, decorated with fishing flies. But for hunting in the woods, Fly Rod knew better. Years earlier she had followed deer tracks and taken aim on the gray shape of a deer, only to glimpse a flash of red an instant before pulling the trigger. Moments later, when she saw that the gray was the jacket of a friend, and the red a glimpse of his guide's hat, Fly Rod realized how easily a tragic error could be made. In a column she later explained:

> [That experience] gives me the chills as I recall the event and think what might have been . . . Then we talked over the danger of a hunter wearing such a color in the woods during the hunting season and I have never since been hunting unless I wore a red hat or sweater.

So as she dressed for a fourth day hunting for her caribou, Crosby donned her favorite scarlet sweater and cap. As usual she wore a long skirt that ended slightly above her sturdy boots. The year before she had caused a huge stir at the National Sportsmen's Exhibition at Madison Square Garden by wearing a hunting skirt a scandalous *seven* inches off the floor. Hosting the Maine exhibit, she demonstrated the use of artificial flies and showed off the fish and game available in Maine. Fly Rod was the talk of the show, but in newspapers from Alabama to Montana, her skirt length made almost as many headlines as her fly fishing.

Cummings and Crosby continued searching the ground and woods. Suddenly, they spotted three caribou well ahead of them, nibbling on a patch of gray moss. The smallest of the three began heading back toward them, nibbling as he edged slowly closer. Cummings whispered, "Now don't get nervous there, you've got him!" But after trying for two years, Crosby did not want just any caribou. She wanted a full-antlered buck. If she couldn't get that, she would wait.

With a steady gaze, Crosby watched and waited for the caribou to double back for more moss and come into rifle range. The largest of the three was a buck with a magnificent rack of antlers. He would be perfect! With exquisite patience she waited, perfectly still, for the right moment.

As the caribou came within 200 yards, Crosby raised her Winchester rifle. It was a 38.55 caliber given to her by the Winchester company in recognition of her sporting prowess. Ignoring her rapidly beating heart, Crosby sat perfectly still . . . 150 yards . . . 140 yards . . . 130 yards. . . . Come on . . . a little closer, her mind pleaded.

Just as the group reached 125 yards they startled, perhaps suddenly aware of the danger. But Crosby was ready and at that moment she fired. The buck fell, then struggled to get back on his feet as the other two bounded out of range to safety. Crosby shot again and the caribou was still. Ecstatic, she rushed over to inspect her prize. She had finally succeeded. On December 10, 1897, Cornelia "Fly Rod" Crosby became the first woman to shoot a caribou legally in the state of Maine.

Within days Crosby had delivered the caribou to be mounted and planned some special furniture for her home. With typical modesty she didn't write about the hunt in her column for months. But in her hometown of Phillips, she shared both the story and the bounty, later saying, "all my friends within reach dined on venison."

A serious knee injury the following year led to damage that eventually limited Fly Rod's ability to explore the woods, but not her ability to promote Maine through her writing. She continued to write until the 1920s, compiling hundreds of articles and columns extolling the virtues of Maine not only for the "lords of creation" but for ladies also, as she did at the close of this August 1901 column for *Field & Stream:*

> How I wish more of you ladies would leave the party dresses at home, for winter's gayety [sic] if you choose, but take the short skirt, the sensible boot, and come to Maine. I'll teach you to fish and tell you where to enjoy life. Come to Maine.

In the sitting room of her home in Phillips, surrounded by mementos and photos of her years fly fishing, Fly Rod would rest her leg on a unique ottoman. Covered in caribou hide, it was raised off the floor by the feet of her prize caribou, whose head and antlers looked down from where they were mounted on the wall.

The caribou herd migrated to Canada the following year and have never returned. Despite several recent attempts, wildlife experts have not been able to reintroduce a herd successfully into Maine. According to official records, Fly Rod Crosby was not only the first woman, but may have been the last hunter ever to be successful hunting caribou in Maine.

NOTE: At the Annual Sportsmen's Exposition in New York's Madison Square Garden, Fly Rod passed out Maine spruce gum packaged in wood boxes shaped like small log cabins.

A Sucker
Every Minute
· 1898 ·

The news coverage of Lubec's Klondike began with a short item listed under Washington County in the January 5, 1898, edition of the *Portland Transcript* over 200 miles away:

> It is reported that gold and silver were taken from the sea water at North Lubec at the rate of $2 worth per hour, a few days ago, and that the company intends putting in 200 machines of that capacity.

In the late 1800s, dreams of gold spread all across the country. Many remembered the 1849 California Gold Rush, and more recently, adventurous Mainers had traveled to the Alaskan gold fields. Maine had its first gold strike in Madrid, Maine, in 1854, and significant finds of gold and silver were made in Acton and other small Maine towns. Speculators rushed to Maine, eager to dig their fortune, but with the *Transcript* story came a new possibility. If straightened, Maine's coastline would stretch 3,478 miles. So, if the ocean's water could be harvested of gold and silver, Maine's fortune would be almost limitless. Most Mainers were cautious and waited for more news.

The preceding November, the Reverend Prescott F. Jernegan and Charles E. Fisher had incorporated the Electrolytic

Marine Salts Company (EMS Co.) in the Portland law office of Levy Turner. The two partners then sold a secret formula to the company in exchange for 45 percent of the proceeds from stock sales. Jernegan supposedly had been conducting over 200 experiments using electricity, chemistry, and quicksilver in a method designed to extract gold from seawater. With Fisher's help he planned to establish the EMS Co. along Maine's Passamaquoddy Bay and begin making his fortune extracting gold.

Jernegan arrived at Lubec explaining that the huge rise and fall of tides at the point of Passamaquoddy Bay where it narrowed was ideal for maximizing the tidal currents for the extraction of gold. He was a young Baptist minister from a prominent Martha's Vineyard family. His communication skills, background, and respectable image inspired trust that would prove most helpful in overcoming the natural skepticism toward his venture. Charles Fisher was an old friend of Jernegan's—he also came from an old Martha's Vineyard family and brought some very useful skills for the EMS enterprise, not all of which were public knowledge. Work began on a demonstration site and a larger plant. By the time of the January *Transcript* article, the demonstration site was up and running, and word began to spread. According to the May 11 *Transcript:*

> Nine shipments have been made from the works of the Electrolytic Marine Salts Mining Co. of East Lubec, to date. They are said to have average about $1000 apiece in value.

EMS Co. invested a great deal of time and money in the town as they began building Plant Number 1. They built a watering trough for horses and factory and support buildings, and they brought the first telephone and electric systems to town. They even paid half the cost of building a new steel bridge across the canal for the town and finished the interior work on the Lubec Baptist Church. It was well known about town that workmen were held to a high moral standard, even being required to participate in regular Sunday prayer. All of this helped reassure the townspeople and gave the entire company an air of respectability. By the end of May, the normally skeptical locals had been won over, as the *Lubec Herald* (May 24) commented: "We believe that time will prove these gentlemen of the EMS Co. to be staunch friends and people who will take a warm interest in the welfare of the Town." Soon even the locals were digging cash out of their favorite hiding spots to get in on the venture that promised them easy wealth for the price of a share of EMS stock.

The first stock sold for $1.00 a share. Over 350,000 shares in the first offering sold out in just three days, mostly to Boston investors. Jernegan counted on the plant's remote location to prevent most investors from visiting. But despite the distance, some did travel to the Lubec plant for a personal tour, determined to see the miraculous extraction with their own eyes.

Jernegan led investors down the stairs and through a door into a room beneath the wharf. The visitors were shown 30-inch boxes containing a battery, some mercury, and a secret combination of other chemicals. Jernegan would lower the "accumulator" box deep into the salt water. As the box disappeared from sight into the deep water, he explained that the depth provided optimal current flow to the accumulator at high tide and provided extra protection from theft. Now visitors had to wait for the tides to pour through while the accumulators extracted the precious metals from the salt water and trapped them inside the box.

Twenty-four hours later, they watched as the box was lifted out of the water and opened to reveal what had been extracted since it was lowered. Gazing at the small but valuable chunks of gold and silver, shareholders were convinced they actually had seen the process work. The demonstration of one box was impressive, and knowing that Plant Number 1 had 250 boxes working daily excited the investors. Hearing that the planned Plant Number 2 would have an additional 5,000 boxes convinced many to rush back to purchase even more stock. Their excited tales of what they had seen made them perfect spokesmen for recruiting even more investors. By July an estimated 2.4 million shares of stock had been sold to investors all over the East Coast, although it would later be found that money had been received to that point for only 900,000 shares.

By now almost 800 men were at work in the factory or constructing the many buildings for Plant Number 1 and the proposed Plant Number 2. Late in July Fisher left, ostensibly on business. No one thought anything about that, but a few days later, Jernegan could not be found on the site. A visit to Jernegan's home revealed the entire family had gone, taking their personal belongings as well. Further investigation found that all of the company account books and ledgers were also missing. Suspicion turned to alarm. Almost fifty years later, Richard Larrabee, one of the young carpenters working on the site, recalled the day the scheme crumbled:

> About 2 o'clock fellers come around and told us
> workmen it had folded up. They paid off all the men,
> but the investors lost every cent they put into it.
> Biggest swindling scheme we ever had in Maine!

The July 29, 1898, *Hartford Courant* ran a headline announcing "The Bubble Burst," and in three days the stock sank from $1.40 to 30 cents per share. A warrant for the arrest of Prescott Jernegan "on the charge of obtaining money under false pretenses" was issued in Boston on July 30. On July 31 all work stopped at the plant. Following the story, early in August, the *Transcript* noted: "Jernegan left New York for Havre, France, several days ago taking with him about $100,000 or more . . . A demand will be made on the French authorities for his arrest."

The Pinkerton Detective Agency had been hired to investigate and find Jernegan and Fisher. Fisher was never located, but Jernegan was found in France where a Boston reporter interviewed him in Havre. Jernegan feigned innocence, claiming he was trying to locate Fisher, who had taken valuable company records. He justified the money he had with him as necessary for new equipment he hoped to purchase. Jernegan gave no explanation for why he and his family were traveling under the name Louis Sinclair. Unfortunately, French authorities had not received the proper paperwork to take Jernegan into custody, and he slipped away. The August papers were full of conflicting reports of events in Maine and France, plus rumors as to Fisher's location. Some still clung to hope. Again the *Transcript* (August 10) reported: "Several stockholders are still confident that gold can be obtained from sea salt, and say that the plant at Lubec should be kept running."

The papers continued to follow the story into the fall as more and more evidence of fraud piled up. How had the hoax succeeded in the demonstrations? News that Charles Fisher was a skilled underwater diver led many to believe that he had been putting the gold into the boxes during the night, out of sight in the deep water. Test after test was performed on the Lubec accumulators and the October 12 *Transcript* reported the disappointing results:

The end of the gold from salt water scheme with which "Rev." P. F. Jernegan was concerned at Lubec would appear to have been reached, a careful and thorough test of the alleged process having failed completely to show the slightest result.

Most reports suggest that Fisher died in Australia, and that Jernegan was last heard of teaching in the Philippines. He eventually sent between $75,000 and $85,000 back to investors, though he never admitted to any responsibility or even that his process was a hoax. In a strange twist the August 24 *Transcript* reported a rumor that the defunct EMS plant was to be converted for use as a sardine factory. This rumor proved to be true, and the sardine industry was soon bringing Lubec far more wealth than Jernegan's gold scheme had.

Yankee yarns frequently tell tales of gullible visitors from "away" being hoodwinked by wily locals with a scheme. In Lubec natives remember hearing about the time when a man of the cloth came to town and managed to fool people from all over the East Coast with his "gold from seawater" invention. That time, even the locals were taken in by the scam.

Gold from seawater? From a chemical standpoint, there *is* gold in ocean water. However, the gold content is valued only at around $1.50 for an entire ton of seawater. Even with today's technology, the cost of extracting gold in significant quantities continues to be totally impractical. The only gold that has ever come from the waters off North Lubec has come from marketing the sardine brought in by the boats of Passamaquoddy Bay.

Maine Women Make Their Mark

· 1920 ·

Helen Bates stood in the back of an open car speaking to a crowd of almost 2,000 people. The car was draped in flag bunting, and many of the listeners wore the "Votes for Women" buttons that had been handed out. May 14 had been declared National Suffrage Day, and finally, in 1912, the Portland newspapers had begun to report on the regular meetings of the Maine Equal Suffrage Association. As its president Bates had helped mail or hand out box after box of printed information sheets from the National Women's Suffrage Association. Maine's group concentrated on getting out information about their cause, so Bates was pleased to see a few reporters in the crowd. It was hardly a groundswell, but the movement was getting stronger.

That same year, suffragettes presented their case to the state legislature in Augusta. Almost ten years earlier, the legislature had briefly considered a bill allowing women to vote, but it would have limited the extension of the franchise to those who paid taxes. The Equal Suffrage Association wanted no such limits. Passing out "Votes for Women" cards and buttons, they lobbied legislators up and down the halls and prepared to testify. The *Portland Evening Express* reported on their efforts:

No rioting was manifested in their conduct, no cheers were made; there were no songs and no parades. What if they didn't have banners and sky rockets and other fireworks? They were armed with much more effective weapons; they had well prepared speeches, short and concise.

The speeches, however well prepared, were not enough. The bill was approved by the men of the Judiciary Committee and passed in the House, but it failed in the Senate. Women did not get to vote in the elections of 1912. Maine's suffragettes continued to fight. They lobbied for their cause in newspapers and magazines. The elections of 1916 came and went, but still Maine's women did not get to vote. They marched, gave more speeches, and wrote more articles.

In 1918 the United States House of Representatives passed House Joint Resolution 1, proposing a nineteenth amendment to the U.S. Constitution, "extending the right of suffrage to women." It passed in the U.S. Senate the next year. If three-quarters of the current states voted to ratify the amendment, it would become the law of the land. In August 1920 the Maine legislature was preparing to vote. Approval by Maine's legislature would bring the amendment's total close to the required thirty-six. As in many states, there was great controversy, and not just among men. Maine's Governor Carl Milliken tackled the difference of opinion head-on: "It is true that some conservative women shrink from the responsibility of suffrage. On the other hand, many others are willing to accept the responsibility if it is placed upon them. If only one woman in Maine wants to vote, she ought to have the chance."

Percival Baxter, who later became governor, was among those who spoke up, urging fellow representatives to vote for ratifying the suffrage amendment. It was uncomfortably close, seventy-two to sixty-eight, but Maine's legislature did vote to ratify. Just days later, the Tennessee legislature's vote of approval made it official. A proclamation announcing that the Constitutional amendment officially had become law was signed on August 26, in Washington, D.C. That night a double headline topped the *Portland Evening Express:*

Legislature to Meet Next Tuesday to Amend
Law and Permit Women to Vote

Maine's legislators had to hurry. In 1920 presidential elections were held on different dates in different states. Maine's presidential elections were already set for September 13. That left only eighteen days in which to get procedures up and running and to register Maine's new voters. Governor Milliken immediately called for a special session of the legislature.

Not everyone waited for the official sanction of the Maine legislature's special session. Immediately after hearing of the official proclamation in Washington, the chairman of Bangor's Board of Registrars, Colonel William Southard, got out the registration papers. He signed up his wife Gertrude and claimed for her the honor of being the first woman registered to vote under the Nineteenth Amendment. One hundred miles away, seventy-six-year-old church organist Alice Skolfield was registering to vote the same day. She was scheduled to go away on vacation the week of September 13, but when she heard the Nineteenth Amendment was official, she canceled her plans. She would later say that she wasn't about to miss her first chance to vote! A few years later, Maine election officials declared a tie, so Southard and Skolfield share the claim of being first.

The legislature's special session met, and the governor addressed the joint body, urging both unity and speed:

The women of Maine [are] prepared to accept cheerfully and faithfully discharge the new responsibilities thus placed upon them. And Maine men, whether they have previously advocated equal suffrage or not, desire that the process of placing women voters on full equality with men be not only ungrudging and complete, but as prompt as possible.

The legislature agreed, quickly voting official approval. In no time lines began forming outside city halls and at the homes of village clerks across the state. In the first six days that registration offices were open, 6,685 women were registered in Portland alone.

In barely a week election day arrived. Women flocked to the polls in such numbers that one newspaper reported, "At one time there were 11 women within the inclosure [sic] and the single man voter in this group appeared sadly out of place." The total vote was extremely large in all wards of the city of Portland, and cities and villages all over Maine saw similarly large turnouts.

Reporters noted the absence of "frivolity" at polling places. "The women voters were fully aware of the importance of their role in today's election . . . they went about casting their first ballot with serious mien." Having waited years for the right to vote, they wasted no time. Seeing that they marked their ballots more quickly than male voters, newspapers explained, "it was indicated that their minds had been made up as to which of the candidates would get their votes before they entered the polling places."

Young women eagerly marked their ballots, excited to be in on the beginning of a new age in election history. Older women were more subdued, conscious of how long the fight had been going on. Many had worked most of their adult lives for this, not certain they would live to see the day come. Nothing would stop them from voting now. Women with automobiles drove miles away, picking up anyone in rural areas who had no way of getting to the polls. Others walked. The news picked up the story of Nancy Skillings, reportedly the oldest to vote in the election. She had no intention of missing her chance to vote and "walked from home to the voting place some distance away and returned the same way." Skillings was ninety-four years old.

After the election Maine papers reported "one of the biggest Republican sweeps in a state election." The state contests were amazingly consistent. All sixteen counties voted Republican. Every single state senator was a Republican. Almost every representative was also a Republican.

The presidential elections of 1920 were the first to include the votes of women from every state. With the late August enactment of the Nineteenth Amendment, the speedy action of the Maine legislature, and the September 13 election date, Maine's women were first. Election experts were eager to see the impact of America's new voting constituency. The turnout and enthusiasm shown by Maine's women voters set a trend repeated in state after state later that fall. The actual vote set a trend also. The final presidential vote in Maine was Warren G. Harding (R) 136,355 and James M. Cox (D) 58,961. When Harding's running mate, Calvin Coolidge, saw the vote totals in Maine, he was ecstatic, sending Harding a telegram that said given the Maine results, they were as good as elected. He was right. Maine's September returns accurately predicted the final outcome in the election of 1920.

Off the Trail
·1939·

Cold, misty clouds swirled around twelve-year-old Donn Fendler. Only minutes before, he had left his friend Henry Condon below Mount Katahdin's Baxter Peak. Henry and Donn had raced ahead of their climbing party to reach the summit, and they had been waiting for the others before heading down together. Impatient, Donn started down the trail alone, the clouds quickly closing in behind him. The trail seemed rougher than he remembered going up. Each time he thought he saw someone ahead, it turned out to be just cloud-covered rocks. Donn assumed the tableland plateau was just ahead. He kept going but soon was clambering over patches of large rocks and getting poked and scratched by puckerbush points. He knew the trail didn't have such large rocks or these puckerbushes. He began to feel nervous. Coming up Hunt Trail earlier, white daubs of paint had marked the trail, but Donn couldn't see a single marked rock or tree. He was definitely off the trail.

He shouted.

There was no reply.

Earlier that morning Donn, his father, and four others had left their campsite and begun the climb in warm sunshine. Maine was cooler than his home in Rye, New York, but in the clouds and winds near the rocky peaks of mile-high Mount Katahdin, it was hard to believe this was the middle of July. It felt more like winter. Sleet began to fall, forming a thin coat on his jacket and quickly soaking his dungarees. Hours passed.

Donn kept walking. He was alone on Maine's highest mountain and he was lost.

Suddenly, Donn's feet broke through a puckerbush patch and he began falling. Quickly, he grabbed a handful of the sharp branches and held on. He could see 20 or 30 feet down to the sharp and jagged rocks at the bottom of the hole. Praying that the roots would hold, Donn dug in his toes and slowly pulled himself up to safety. Shaken badly by the close call, Donn panicked and began running back and forth up the hill, crying and shouting. Frantic, he crashed over rocks and through brush. Eventually spent, he sat on a rock and tried to think more clearly. He needed a plan to survive and to get back to his family.

When Donn hadn't returned to the campsite by late afternoon, a search party was organized and began scouring the trail. The searchers struck off, sure that they would return with Donn in just a few hours. Reaching the tree line just after dark, they scanned the valley below. One light at the base camp would mean Donn was still missing. Two lights would mean to come back. Clouds had already begun closing in around the search party, obscuring the base and any signal. If there were thick clouds at this level, conditions would be much worse where Donn was. The searchers pushed themselves even harder.

As freezing rain and darkness fell, searchers made steady progress up the mountain. They headed for the tableland area where Donn had first gotten separated from his group. Using iron handholds and footholds, they carefully negotiated the rocks. The climb normally takes two and a half hours, but fueled by their desperate concern, the searchers managed to get there in just two. Their flashlight beams disappearing quickly in the fog, they worked their way systematically across and around the area where Donn had been last seen.

Allen Bulmer of Revere, Massachusetts, was one of the searchers that Monday and later described the conditions in the *Revere Journal:*

In all my life, I have never been in a more desolate place. The wind was blowing 40 miles an hour or more. The temperature hovered around 40 degrees, although I would swear it was less. My hands had grown numb from the cold and I swapped my flashlight from one hand to the other. Rain and sweat ran down my face. My shoes, stockings, and pants were covered with mud from searching through rain-drenched grass and rain-drenched brush. My feet began to ache. My legs ached. My back, my knees— I ached all over. My heart set up a terrific pounding in my ears. I was wretched. . . . The sides [of the rocks] became steeper and seemed to fall away on each side into mist-filled bottomless pits. Cliffs of ugly rock rose up straight 350 feet and here and there large patches of snow clung. I shuddered to think of the little lad's possible fate.

The next morning, local guides, woodsmen, and state police resumed their search, but those who knew Katahdin's rugged terrain feared the boy would not be found alive. Maine newspapers reported the story and expressed doubt a child could have survived the night's storm unprotected.

But Donn did survive the night. Knowing it was important to remain calm, he tried to remember what he had learned as a Boy Scout. He knew that to stay still in the open was to risk freezing to death, so he kept moving. Sometimes wandering in circles, he prayed for courage and protection. Donn blamed himself for his predicament, for not having stayed with his father and brothers on the hike.

Hours passed.

Exhausted, drenched, and freezing, Donn needed a safe, dry place to sleep, but he had to get out of the barren rocks above the timberline, through the rough brush, and into the woods below. When he reached the trees, conditions were less severe, but it was still wet and cold. Donn finally curled up between the roots of a large tree, scraping moss into a thin mat. He put his sneakers with his dungarees under an old tree trunk to keep them from getting wetter and noticed both had been shredded by the sharp rocks. He wound his shirt around his head, pulled his fleece-lined jacket down over his legs, and cried himself to sleep.

The next day, Donn again relied on his Boy Scout training. He had to stay calm. He might be able to find edible berries. He should look for clear, running water. If he could find that, he would have water to drink and could follow the stream down the mountain. Surely someone would find him long before that.

Five hundred men and boys searched Mount Katahdin's trails above the timberline for five long days. No one thought Donn could have gotten below the tree line that first terrible night. Loggers from timber crews, men from the paper mills, the Forest Service, and eventually the National Guard all joined the search. But for those five days, no one ever looked below the timberline. Bloodhounds searched until their paws were cut so badly they had to quit. By Saturday night search crews finally began searching the forests below the timberline. By Monday Donn had been gone a week, and most searchers had given up and gone home. Only a small group of volunteers continued to look for him. Newspapers no longer carried daily updates. How could a twelve-year-old boy with no protection, no food, and no experience possibly survive all alone for over a week?

Tuesday afternoon Nelson McMoarn was working outside his remote log cabin camp along the Penobscot River's East Branch. He heard what sounded like a screech owl and looked up. Far on the opposite shore he saw a small, nearly naked figure, crawling along a log, yelling and waving its arms.

McMoarn answered Donn's weak cries, and Donn knew he was saved. The next thing he remembered was a big man who "didn't say much—just shook his head and picked me up." McMoarn quickly notified authorities. In the morning Donn was taken by canoe down the Penobscot River 14 miles to Grindstone, the nearest town, then by ambulance to a Bangor hospital.

When newspapers all across the country reported his return, Donn became a celebrity, and telegrams poured in from all over. He recovered completely and years later wrote a book detailing his adventure (*Lost on a Mountain in Maine*). Donn Fendler credits God and his Boy Scout training for the faith and level head that enabled him to survive his ordeal. He still receives letters from readers who are full of questions about his adventure. Fendler also visits schools, mesmerizing young fans with his amazing story.

Experts later recreated Donn's roundabout route. Early during the nine days he was lost, his pants and shoes had been totally shredded. Donn had encountered deer and bears and had been tormented by black flies and other insects. He was covered with bruises, bites, and infected cuts. Surviving on only berries and stream water, Donn was emaciated, with only fifty-eight pounds left on his four-foot-seven-inch frame. But throughout his ordeal, Donn had always trusted God to take care of him, praying often for help. He never gave up. He tried catching fish and starting a fire with two pieces of iron he found. Finally, he found a brook, which became the stream that eventually led him down to the East Branch of the Penobscot River and McMoarn's remote camp. Donn had walked at least 96 miles, perhaps as far as 130 miles. Alone in some of Maine's most challenging terrain, twelve-year-old Donn Fendler had survived.

Silent Night
· 1944 ·

H. Fenton Shaw was worried. He had over a hundred acres of potatoes planted on his Aroostook County farm. They would soon be ready to dig, and he had no one but his family to help with the harvest. Aroostook County normally employed 32,000 workers each year to harvest its enormous potato crop. In the year and a half since Pearl Harbor, thousands of workers had left northern Maine. Many had enlisted to fight in World War II. Those who couldn't fight found other ways to help the war effort. Many found high-paying jobs at the shipyards in Portland. Shaw knew that the produce from his farm and the lumber from his woodlot were also important to the war effort, but he needed help.

Shaw had heard about an unusual opportunity and discussed it with his wife. On July 1, 1944, a camp with 299 prisoners of war sent from Europe and transferred from Camp Edwards in Massachusetts had opened in Houlton. They were mostly a mix of German Afrika Korps veterans and Wehrmacht troops captured after the Normandy invasion. Since July more POWs had arrived on the Bangor and Aroostook Railroad and had been trucked from downtown Houlton to the camp. Now there were almost a thousand prisoners at Camp Houlton. Local farmers and lumbermen had been told that prisoners could be assigned to work details in the area.

Some Mainers were nervous. Would the prisoners do good work? Would they try to escape to Canada? What if they set fires to destroy the lumber? Most important, weren't these prisoners the enemy? Before capture, these men had been part of the army that was killing and wounding young American soldiers.

Shaw and his wife had heard the concerns. They understood the anger and the fear. The Shaws chose to take a different view. Recalling it forty years later, Fenton Shaw said, "I figured I had the privilege of showing them that we were human over here on this side of the ocean." The Shaws would give the prisoners a chance to help. Others agreed, and soon prisoners were given regular work assignments on farms and woodlots in the Houlton area.

Shaw began making the 40-mile trip between his Easton farm and the camp in Houlton. Each day, he trucked twenty or thirty prisoners to help with the potato harvest. Digging potatoes is hard work, and the prisoners, who had no experience, weren't able to pick potatoes clean enough as their hands became scraped and sore. Sizing up the problem, Shaw went to a local store and, with his own money, purchased work gloves for each of the men. When officials at the camp saw what a difference it made, all of the other work crews assigned to potato farms were issued gloves.

Farm work was popular among the prisoners. They enjoyed using tractors and other modern farm equipment. Prisoners dug potatoes, picked beans, and shucked peas. That fall the local Birds Eye frozen food plant operated twenty-four hours a day freezing and packing peas and beans. That size harvest would have been impossible without the help of the German prisoners. Maine families were painfully aware of what the prisoners had been doing before arriving in Maine, but slowly they began to get to know the people who were working in their fields.

Each prisoner was allotted a daily lunch ration. For those on work details, the camp provided a simple box lunch and water. Shaw knew how much energy was expended working all day in a field, and he and his wife began bringing big pots of soup or stew to the field for the men. They would eat with the men and soon got to know the young men as individuals. Passing around big pots of coffee, they listened as prisoners talked about life in the camps.

The camp was 1,350 feet by 650 feet, and prisoners were housed in long barracks, surrounded by a double barbed wire fence guarded with six machine-gun towers. Inside the camp there was an infirmary with both American and German doctors and dentists. Each day began and ended with head counts, followed in the morning by sick call. Prisoners worked up to ten hours a day, but with up to two hours of travel each way to their work sites, there wasn't much time left to relax after work. Sundays were free. Prisoners were given a basic pay of $3.00 each month. Officials had determined a production quota for each work assignment. If a prisoner could meet the daily quota of cords cut or bushels picked, he could earn an additional 80 cents per day.

Prisoners were paid in canteen credits. Houlton prisoners averaged about $14 per month with their field work. With these credits they could purchase cigarettes (13 cents a pack), candy bars (5 cents), beer (25 cents), and other sundries. They looked forward to their canteen shopping, and when Shaw's men occasionally did not meet their work quota, he would come up with excuses to give the prison officials so they would be excused from the quota and given their full pay.

Shaw's 240 acres was not all farmland. After the potatoes were all in and winter approached, Shaw turned his attention to his woodland acres. Suffering from the same labor shortage as the farms, Maine's pulpwood and lumbering operations were 40 percent below normal in 1944. Supply was down to 50 percent of what was needed for the war effort. Lumber was desperately needed to rebuild ports and for manufacturing crates for war material. In Van Buren, Maine, the biggest lumber mill east of the Mississippi normally produced 100,000 feet of lumber a day. Wood from Shaw's farm was part of the more than 25 million board feet of pulpwood that was floated down to Van Buren each year. Once again POWs were assigned to help fill the manpower gap. Shaw arranged with the Houlton camp to have another forty POWs help cut the pulpwood on his farm.

Most Maine woodlots are very remote, and winter workers have to deal with freezing cold and deep snow. There were very few escape attempts. Rudi Richter, looking back on his days as a POW in the Maine woods, said, "We had been told the forest was populated by wild Indians who would not hesitate to kill escaping prisoners. We had no reason not to believe these stories." The few who made headlines for attempting escape were captured quickly or turned themselves in when faced with the cold and rugged terrain. As Shaw said, "Maine prisoners were shown maps of the big Maine woods and told they could try to escape if they wanted to, but where would they go?"

Shortly before Christmas, Shaw and his wife discussed the holiday and what they could do for the forty-two prisoners they had come to know. During their lunches with the men, the Shaws had learned about German holiday customs, and they could hear how much the men missed their homes. Christmas trees were a tradition in Germany before they were in America. So the Shaws began by allowing the men to cut down several small evergreen trees to take back to the camp and decorate.

The Shaws also learned that the men were used to a two-day Christmas holiday. The prison camp was giving only Christmas Day off. Fenton Shaw came up with a plan. The day before Christmas, he phoned the prison camp and told officers in charge that he was terribly sorry, but his truck had broken down. He just couldn't seem to get it working, so he would not be able to pick up the men to come to work that day.

After calling the camp, Shaw's family spent the day preparing a special surprise for the young men who worked his land. They put together a Christmas stocking for each worker, filled with foods hard to get in the camp: apples, oranges, nuts, and, of course, candy bars. The family loaded all forty-two stockings into their car, climbed in, and headed up to Houlton. When they reached the camp, they handed out the stockings to the men who had begun as unknown enemies but were now familiar faces, with individual stories and personalities. The prisoners had not expected such generosity and had no gifts to give in return. Then a single voice began . . . *"Stille Nacht."* A second voice joined in . . . *"Heilige Nacht."* Another voice joined the song, and then another, until all of the prisoners were singing. The words were German, but the beauty and emotion in the melody of "Silent Night" knew no barrier. The fears, animosities, and hardships of war were put on hold. The compound lights and barbed wire were forgotten as the notes of the familiar Christmas carol seemed to hang suspended in the cold Maine air.

The POWs continued to work for the Shaws throughout the war. When the war ended, Shaw gathered all those who had worked on his farm for a photo. Grouped together in their knit stocking caps and woolen shirts, some held the wood saws they had used. Shaw had a copy made for each of the men. By May 26, 1946, the POWs from all of Maine's camps had been returned home. Many carried memories of Americans who had treated enemy prisoners with respect and often kindness.

Fenton Shaw's treatment of the German prisoners was a testament to people's ability to be fair even in the face of war. Neither Shaw nor the forty-two men who worked his land would ever forget their days spent harvesting pulpwood and potatoes. Simple pairs of gloves for scratched, sore hands. Warm cups of coffee and noontime stew shared in cold fields and sitting on stumps in snowy woods. Small Christmas pines. Fruit-filled stockings. And the simple notes of a Christmas song.

Cheating the Sea: The Wreck of the *Oakey L. Alexander*

· 1947 ·

Captain Raymond Lewis watched from the wheelhouse as a huge wave snatched one of the *Oakey L. Alexander*'s two lifeboats and dislodged it from its moorings. Seconds later, the lifeboat disappeared into the darkness in a gust of ferocious wind. The *Oakey L. Alexander* was fighting its way through mountainous seas off the coast of Maine in a storm that had grown worse with every hour. At fifty-three, Lewis was an experienced captain from Boston, Massachusetts, used to rough seas and winter storms. But as he fought to keep the ship on course, Lewis knew this was no ordinary winter storm.

The *Oakey L. Alexander* was a 395-foot collier built in 1916 for the Pocahontas Steamship Company. As flagship of the fleet, she was named for the president of the company. On this trip she carried a 8,200-ton cargo of coal and a crew of thirty-one, including sixteen from Maine. She had steamed into a storm that seemed determined to show its control over everyone's fate. As wave after wave engulfed the ship, it seemed like more than steel and men could survive. Then the second, and last, lifeboat was lifted by a wave, smashed into the deck aft of the bridge, and lay useless. Captain Lewis ordered full steam as the ship prepared to enter Portland Harbor. It was 4:00 A.M., Tuesday, March 4, 1947.

Onshore, communities all along the coast had lost electrical power. Portland's Head Light lighthouse keeper, William Lockhart, turned on the emergency generator to keep the foghorn and lighthouse beacon working through the storm. Thirty-foot to forty-foot waves broke on the rocks. The lighthouse at Portland Head in Cape Elizabeth stands over 80 feet above the rocky promontory, yet spray from the waves was shooting more than 150 feet into the air—the equivalent of a fifteen-story building. The lighthouse's fog bell was mounted in the engine room building, a few feet from the lighthouse. Lockhart watched in awe as the sea thundered through the space between the engine room and the tower, making even that small distance impassible. Waves smashed the lighthouse's fog bell, and winds gusted to eighty miles per hour, the worst storm Lockhart had seen in his sixteen years in the Light Service. Battling with the noise of the surf and wind was the constant pelting of rocks coming "at bullet velocity."

Onboard the *Oakey L. Alexander,* First Assistant Engineer Arthur Bradley came on duty. His shift in the engine room began at 4:00 A.M., just as the *Alexander* headed for Portland Harbor. Less than an hour later, "I felt a terrific jar. It sounded like a heavy sea, not like the ship hitting anything." The captain later testified that two huge waves split the bow. Seaman Rodney Turner, twenty, of East Boothbay, Maine, was on watch and eyewitness to what happened next. "For a few minutes, the bow moved up and down, like it was elastic. The bow held together for a few minutes and then let go with a terrific noise." Over a third of the ship had been torn off at her bow. With 5,000 pounds of coal in the bow holds, 165 feet of the forward section broke away and disappeared into the darkness. It was 4:46 A.M.

Captain Lewis rang an emergency alarm, ordered an SOS, and assembled the crew. After assessing the damage, he ordered slow speed ahead and told the crew he was going to try to beach the *Alexander* on High Head in Cape Elizabeth. Lewis kept the stern of the ship to the waves to reduce roll as much as possible. He didn't know if they would make the beach or not. Lewis promised the crew he would warn them three minutes before they hit the rocks. He knew that, by deliberately beaching the ship, the crew might have a chance to survive. "No one will ever have a crew as calm as mine. Every man stood by his post," Lewis later testified. "We rode the sea to the ledges much like a surfboard."

Engineer Bradley said, "The captain called down [to the engine room] and told us we were headed for the rocks. We were on our way up the ladder to the deck when we hit with scarcely a jar. I said my prayers, for I knew if the ledges punctured her sides, we would not be here to tell about it."

The bottom scraped along the rocks of High Head, just outside the mouth of Portland Harbor, and the ship took a list to port. It was 5:59 A.M.

Chief Warrant Boatswain Earle Drinkwater was commanding officer of the responding U.S. Coast Guard Lifeboat Station. His six-man crew rushed to the scene and saw the grounded collier separated from safety by 150 yards of wild surf. The crew was huddled on deck near the bridge. Their best hope was to be taken off the ship by breeches buoy, a basketlike chair built into a life ring and attached to ropes. The ropes are used like a pulley to haul the basket back and forth, rescuing only one person at a time. But first they had to get the initial line out to the ship.

It had been twenty-two years since Drinkwater had used a Lyle gun to fire a line for a breeches buoy. Now he had to do it with pinpoint accuracy in winds gusting up to sixty miles per hour. With "the cool hand and steady aim of a veteran coast guardsmen," Drinkwater waited for the right moment and then fired. His very first attempt landed aboard the *Alexander,* where the crew caught it and quickly fastened it to the highest point they could reach. "I guess I had very good luck. But you never forget how to fire a line once you have been taught properly," Drinkwater explained later, downplaying his accomplishment. The Coast Guardsmen on shore rigged the tackle and lines, attached the breeches buoy, and started pulling it out to the ship. Now the painstaking rescue could begin.

The first one into the breeches buoy was David Rogers of Virginia, who at eighteen was the youngest crewman on board. The line was twisted and a bit slack, and he was dunked in the icy surf between the ship and the shore several times. Rogers said he took a chance in going over first but wasn't nervous until he got ashore and looked back at the crippled ship and the churning surf. "All hands are safe," he informed the Coast Guard as he was helped out of the basket. Crowds of onlookers had gathered to watch the rescue, and the first cheer went up. It was 8:07 A.M.

Next was Radio Operator Connelly, who had sent the SOS that had signaled the Coast Guard. A young woman onlooker screamed when Connelly was swallowed by the surf. When he reappeared, the crowd cheered. Over and over, the buoy made the trip from ship to shore. One more seaman was soaked by a sudden dip, but as the lines were held taut, the remaining twenty-nine crewmen made the crossing without ever touching the waves. Captain Lewis made the last trip and joined his rescued crew on the beach. They were all safe. It was 10:00 A.M.

Twelve of the rescued crewmen were taken by car to the Portland Seamen's Friend Society on Fore Street. They were given hot coffee, a light lunch, outfitted with shoes and clothes, and offered phones to let relatives know of their rescue. Not one crew member had needed immediate medical attention, though two who were dunked later received treatment for exposure.

People who had come out to watch the rescue came back at low tide to climb down the rocks for a close-up view. The wreck lay broadside to the rocky beach, and waves continued to pound into her open bow. That night the Coast Guard's searchlights and men stood watch over the beached vessel, and as the full moon reflected off the white foam of the surf, the *Oakey L. Alexander* looked like a ghost ship.

The Coast Guard Marine Inspection Board of Inquiry heard two days of testimony and even rode out by launch to board the beached *Alexander*. The ship was a shambles from the storm damage and the constant beating of the waves since beaching. All the coal had disappeared, washed out of the holds, and only a few items were salvaged from the crews' quarters. The board closed its investigation with high praise for the *Oakey L. Alexander*'s Captain Lewis:

> You exhibited the highest degree of seamanship in saving the lives of the entire crew in accordance with your duties under your license as master, and your acts were highly meritorious.

Looking back, Captain Lewis called the destruction of both lifeboats a "blessing in disguise." A safe launch at sea would have been next to impossible in the storm, and "once away it would have been impossible to land the boats safely," given the dangerous breakers and the rocky shore.

Meteorologists later determined that wind velocities during that March storm surpassed the velocity of winds in the disastrous hurricane of 1938. Ships all along the Maine coast struggled to survive. The captain of the 130-foot *Portland Lightship* was awake for seventy-two hours as waves sent water down the ship's smokestack and snapped the chain to the lightship's 5,000-pound anchor. The lightship drifted 4 miles off course as its anchor chain dragged over shoals and rocks.

The Canadian freighter *Novadoc* was not so lucky. The last reports from the ship's master stated that bulkheads had been damaged, a hatch had broken off and been carried away in the winds, and that they were disabled 22 miles off Portland and needed assistance. Flares were sighted, but neither the vessel nor its crew of twenty-five were ever found.

But for the crew of the *Oakey L. Alexander,* their rescuers, and the thousands who watched the drama unfold, it was a morning of triumph. This was a time when luck joined with man's courage, training, and ingenuity. This was a morning when, together, they cheated the sea.

In This Corner...
· 1965 ·

Despite the sunshine and spring weather, schoolboys in Lewiston, Maine, were happy to be inside Saint Dominic's ice rink. Members of a championship ice hockey team, the boys expected to be on the ice every day until summer vacation. But three hours south of Lewiston, boxing promoter Sam Michael was planning a different kind of power play for Saint Dominic's ice rink. Michael was meeting with other boxing officials in Boston, Massachusetts, and they had a problem.

The long-awaited title rematch between Muhammad Ali and Sonny Liston was in trouble. Fans had been itching for a rematch ever since the previous year, when champion Sonny Liston had lost the heavyweight title to a young, brash fighter named Cassius Clay. Liston failed to come out of his corner in the seventh round of the Miami, Florida, fight. After that February win, Clay again made news when he took the Muslim name Muhammad Ali. The rematch had already been postponed once. Now Boston had announced that, because of Massachusetts legal issues, the fight rescheduled for Tuesday, May 26, had to be moved to another state.

Sam Michael stepped forward and volunteered his home state. Suddenly Lewiston, Maine, a struggling milltown of roughly 40,000, had barely two and a half weeks to prepare to host a heavyweight championship fight. That fight would turn out to be one of the most famous—and most debated—in boxing history.

Just a small local youth center, Saint Dominic's had a seating capacity less than 5,000, but the fight promoters didn't object. No one needed to make a lot on ticket sales at the actual fight site. The big money would come from ticket sales for more than one million seats in 258 locations set up for a live satellite broadcast. In fact this would be the first fight beamed live by satellite to fans in Europe.

Sonny Liston arrived in Maine and appeared at the Poland Spring Resort's Mansion House just ten days before the fight. The former heavyweight champion spent Sunday morning horseback riding, playing ball, and walking the golf course. Liston seemed more like a vacationing tourist than a fearsome boxer training for a championship rematch.

The resort's enormous dining room was transformed for Liston's public training sessions, and a week before the fight, spectators in suits and ties sat eight deep. As many as 300 people crowded in to watch Liston drill, skip rope, and spar more than a dozen rounds with different training partners. Local press milked every detail of the training and fight preparations.

Maine was proud and excited to be suddenly in the national spotlight. On Wednesday Sam Michael and three ex-champs were invited to meet in the state capital with Governor John H. Reed. Afterward they were recognized officially by the Maine House of Representatives, held a press conference, and praised the welcome they had received in Maine.

By Saturday the wood floor had been laid over the ice arena, and the 20-foot ring had arrived from Baltimore. At press conferences Liston still seemed relaxed and confident. In his usual pre-fight trash talk, Ali had nicknamed Liston "The Bear." Liston joked with reporters, saying he had heard that there used to be a bounty in Maine for hunting bear, but he felt much better now that all bears in Maine were protected by the state.

On Sunday, May 23, Ali arrived in Maine. Appearing relaxed and jovial, Ali chatted with fans by the Holiday Inn's pool. Later, poking his head out to greet fans gathered below the balcony of his second-floor room, he demonstrated his dancelike shuffle, shadowboxed, and posed for pictures.

Meanwhile, the Maine Boxing Commission met to set the format for the match and to hold a press conference. They chose the referee but would not announce whom it was until the evening of the fight. The ten-point scoring system would be used, with the round winner getting ten points and the loser nine or fewer. There would be a mandatory eight count after a knockdown, and "If a man is dropped for a ten count, even by a low blow, it shall be scored as a knockout. The referee will have complete charge of the fight." It all seemed routine.

Hundreds of unsold high-price tickets were reduced to $25 for local fans when the ticket office opened at ten o'clock on the morning of the fight. In the fight hall workers adjusted banks of massive television lights. Organizers decided the fight clock was too small and replaced it with one that was easier to read from a distance. At 11:30 that morning the two fighters weighed in, and by 1:00 P.M. tiny Auburn–Lewiston airport finished its preparations for a busy night. Electric power lines had been run to the control tower, which had been freshly cleaned and stocked with extra furniture for the four visiting FAA officials sent to handle increased air traffic. In less than four hours, almost seventy aircraft flew in. Looking like an air show, planes were parked everywhere, ready for return flights after the fight.

Finally, the time had come. Both fighters arrived at the arena and went to their locker rooms to get dressed, tape their hands, and warm up. After a few warm-up fights, featuring relatively unknown fighters, the main event was ready to begin. Ring announcer Johnny Addie introduced the two fighters to the 4,280 ticket holders in Lewiston and the widely scattered television audience:

> From Denver, Colorado . . . he's wearing black trunks, he weighs 215¼ pounds, former heavyweight champion and now challenger . . . Sonny Liston.

Liston moved out to the applause and cheers of the crowd.

> From Louisville, Kentucky . . . he's wearing white trunks, he weighs 206 pounds, the heavyweight champion of the world Muhammad Ali.*

Addie introduced the fight referee, former champion Jersey Joe Walcott, who called the two fighters to the center ring. Walcott gave the largely ceremonial instructions ending with the traditional "good luck, shake hands, and come out fighting."

Liston started out trying to pin Ali to the ropes, but Ali danced around, circling left and shuffling lightly, easily evading Liston's almost plodding approach. Liston connected with a weak left to Ali's abdomen but missed a long overhead right. Ali kept moving constantly as Liston missed with a right cross, then he scored with a short right to Liston's head. Liston hit with a short left and a light left jab to Ali's chin, brushing his left elbow, but Ali blocked a left to his torso. Then, barely a minute into the fight, blow-by-blow commentator Russ Hodges described it to radio listeners:

> Sonny feints a right to the midsection, Liston is head bobbing. [Liston] goes to his knees from a punch to the chin. Cassius Clay* is telling him to get up and fight. Jersey Joe Walcott is getting Clay away from [Liston] to get a count . . . . [T]hey can't get Clay away from . . . Liston went *down* from a punch to the chin!

Fight fans were on their feet, stunned by what they were seeing. In all of his professional career, Sonny Liston had never

---

*Announcer Addie used the name Muhammad Ali, but most reporters, including radio announcer Hodges, continued to refer to him as Cassius Clay. Some—including Ali opponents—refused to use Ali's Muslim name for years.

been knocked down; he now lay sprawled on the canvas. His right arm was stretched over his head, his knee bent, and his eyes were glazed. Liston's massive fifteen-inch fists lay harmless, and his famed eighty-four-inch reach touched nothing but canvas. Muhammad Ali stood at Liston's feet, yelling at him to get up and fight. Jersey Joe Walcott rushed forward to get Ali into a neutral corner, but Ali just continued to shout at Liston. Flashbulbs popped all over the arena recording the moment.

Hodges was trying to explain the chaotic scene for his listening audience:

> Jersey Joe Walcott has not started, Jersey Joe Walcott never did start a count. There's nothing but confusion here. [Walcott]'s going over to the judges.

As Walcott was talking to the timekeeper, Liston stood up. The fight resumed just as Walcott came back. It happened so quickly that Hodges never even told his listeners that Liston had gotten up. "Now Clay is on top of Liston, scores a left to the top of Liston's head. Now here comes Jersey Joe Walcott. He says it's all over!"

The boos and jeers from the crowd nearly drowned out the announcer's voice as Ali's hand was raised and a stunned Hodges announced that "Cassius Clay has retained the heavyweight championship of the world." Ali exulted, "I am the greatest. I am the greatest." Addie gave the decision to the angry crowd:

> The timekeeper counted out Liston in one minute of the first round. Said ten seconds had elapsed. The winner by a knockout and still Heavyweight Champion of the World . . . Muhammad Ali."

The fight was over.

Even today, there are three different versions of the length of the fight, depending on whether you used elapsed television time, the "official" time, or the announced time. No matter which time you use, the fight was so brief, the punch so fast, and the knockout so unexpected that it is no surprise there was immediate controversy. Fight films were studied frame by frame to prove that there was a punch and that the knockout was legitimate.

Pictures of Muhammad Ali towering over a sprawling Liston were snapped by professionals and amateurs alike. The contrast of triumph and defeat, pride and humiliation created one of the most memorable images in boxing history. Even people who have never seen a fight, who don't follow the sport, and can't identify the occasion recognize the picture.

For weeks newspapers followed the debates, and a Lewiston editorial accurately predicted: "The echoes of the Clay–Liston fight will continue to ring for months and years." Even today a debate can be started quickly in any sports bar where fight fans gather. Just dare to bring up the night of one of the shortest championship title fights in history. It fueled the legend of Muhammad Ali, one of sport's greatest champions.

If you find yourself in Lewiston, you can still go to the old youth center. Schoolchildren still play ice hockey on the ice rink in May. No sign or plaque is mounted to tell visitors of the excitement that took place May 25, 1965. But occasionally you can find someone who sat in Saint Dominic's that night and saw Sonny Liston's fall. They can tell you the story of a young Muhammad Ali and the night when one of sport's most famous debates began in Lewiston, Maine.

The Last Log Drive
·1976·

Flowing 170 miles from Moosehead Lake to the Atlantic, the Kennebec River drops more than 1,000 feet along the way. From Indian Pond, through Bingham, Solon, Madison, and Skowhegan, veteran log drivers knew the trouble spots. They watched for the midriver obstacles often hidden by water swollen with snowmelt. They memorized the treacherous twists and turns of Misery Stream. They were prepared for the currents at Bombazee Rips, where dangerous white water could suddenly shoot the enormous logs in unexpected directions. If you were a rookie logger, it was a lot to learn.

Leonard "Buster" Violette's rookie log drive was in the 1940s. The seventeen-year-old had no experience with logging, and it wasn't something he could learn in school. There was no gentle mentor to teach the ropes and gradually grant independence. Log driving was learned on the river, and like any other new hand, Buster began on the logs the very first day of work.

He started on what drivers called the "idiot stick," a picaroon used to spike and throw logs washed ashore back into the river. Once he could "pick the rear," he joined the wingmen who worked the edges of the channel. Their job was to keep logs from catching on obstacles in the river or getting tossed ashore. Gradually, Violette learned the many ways to use the long, flexible pole. He could use it to balance like a tightrope walker on the logs or could plant it into the shallows and use it like a vaulting pole to move from log to log or from log to shore.

Booms made of logs fastened together by chains gathered the floating logs into large floating islands called rafts. Rafts then were hooked together and towed by boats across each lake. The logs were then released into the current of the next stretch of river. Rafts often corralled up to fifty acres of massed timber, and each log easily weighed 500 to 900 pounds. Releasing them into a racing current required the ability to think on your feet, literally. Young Violette quickly learned the importance of agility and brute strength, mixed with a healthy dose of daring and nerve. Listening to the veterans' stories of the old days, it was hard to imagine it could be even more dangerous.

On early river drives, logs weren't cut in 4-foot lengths as in Violette's days. They were sent down the river tree-length. Yellow pines were the worst. In great demand for ships, a single tree averaged five tons. Even the spruce and hemlock trees, on an average 40 feet long and a foot square, generally weighed one ton. The huge logs were tossed and thrown by the rapids churning along the length of the Kennebec. Log jams piled up more than 10 feet thick and 5 acres in size, sometimes requiring dynamite to untangle.

One reason for the frequent jams was the sheer volume of logs on the river. The Kennebec River was one of the busiest. At the peak of logging operations, 160 sawmills operated along the Kennebec River, and a single season harvest averaged 150 million logs. A river drive needed 250 to 300 men willing to live away from home for months at a time while working seven days a week from dawn till dusk.

Violette knew only of those days from stories told by the old-time loggers. Buster liked his work and by 1958 was a seasoned veteran. In the mid-1960s he began working year-round, along with master driver Bob "Stubb" Viles and mechanic Carlton Dawes. During the off-season they did maintenance. River drivers still used narrow, flat-bottomed wood boats to maneuver in the rough water. But even those could flip over in the rapids or split in two if they hit a rock in the river, so there were always boats to repair and more boats to build. The motors they now used also required winter maintenance.

Motorboats were not the only change. Many drivers still wore wool shirts and knitted hats, but life jackets and hard hats were becoming common. Two-way radios replaced shouts and flags. Men worked five-day weeks and drove home on weekends. There were many more dams along the river for flood control and hydroelectric power. More people wanted to use the rivers for recreation. A movement began to protect the waterway of rivers and lakes, and in 1971 the Maine legislature passed a law making river driving illegal after 1976.

Buster Violette looked at the logs ready to head down the Kennebec for the Winslow mill. He realized that in the old days no one would have paid much attention to the 1976 drive. With barely 75,000 cords of pulpwood and a crew of only fifty, it was a fraction of the size of past drives. But cameramen and reporters were everywhere. This drive was special. After more than thirty years on the river, this was Buster's last log drive. After almost 300 years, it was the last in the continental United States.

A movie crew shot footage for a documentary about the historic event. Spectators watched the drive along the route. At first the news coverage added some excitement to the routine, but after awhile it was just an annoying distraction. The self-proclaimed "river hogs" went about their work. They had logs to deliver.

As foreman, Buster controlled the drive from Wyman Lake to the Winslow mill. He was everywhere, making sure nothing went wrong. Standing, he piloted his small motorboat along the shore, scanning the work of crews clearing logs thrown up along the banks. He manned a pick pole and helped boat crews guide the logs through the sluice around the Wyman dam. A photographer for *Look* magazine captured a square-jawed, rugged Buster standing astride the sluiceway.

Film crews and newsmen continued snapping pictures everywhere: Hurley Fletcher, hefting a 4-foot log on his shoulder and carrying it to the river edge, and "Bull" McLaughlin pulling on a knitted cap and jumping in to untangle some logs. His wife Barbara had made it especially for this last drive, with a crossed picaroon and pick-pole design on one side and two men in a bateau on the other. Although everyone knew it was the last drive, there was too much work to do to mourn the end of an era. The logs still jammed near Skowhegan, and the men still moved logs into the booms and rafts. Occasionally, it looked like the old days as rivermen stood atop an errant log, using teamwork to pole and "walk" the log out of the shallows back into the channel.

By October the last logs had reached the mill. The last log drive on the Kennebec River was over. Today lumber is hauled in trucks to an ever-shrinking number of mills. Loggers no longer "walk the bubbles" of the Kennebec River. Now life-jacketed tourists ride them in rubber rafts. *Downeast* magazine summarized the change in a May 1981 article:

> Maine's old-time river drivers were the stuff of leg-
> ends: nimble daredevils shod in caulked boots who
> shepherded millions of board feet of pine, spruce,
> and hemlock to lumber mills for wages that in a
> month probably didn't amount to the price of a $50
> ride on one of the modern rubber rafts.

Hurley Fletcher and many of the other men are gone now. Buster and the others shrug off grand phrases about the pass-ing of a lifestyle. They don't consider themselves daredevils, just hardworking men, doing what was needed to get the logs to the mills. The days of massive log drives rafting across lakes and racing down churning water are over, but the mystique of nature and adventure will always be a treasured part of Maine's history.

The Seal of
Approval:
A Governor's Quest
· 1979 ·

From 1979 to 1982, Maine journalists eagerly covered each episode in a fanciful media rivalry between a young Maine governor and a seal named Andre.

Andre was found in Maine's Penobscot Bay, off Robinson's Rock, 4 miles out of Rockport in the spring of 1961. Harry Goodridge, a Rockport tree surgeon and skin diver, spotted the two-day-old abandoned pup. With no mother to feed and protect the baby seal, it wouldn't survive in the wild. Goodridge put the seal in the boat and made his decision. Hours later, Harry bundled the nineteen-pound pup under his slicker as he came up the walk toward home. The softball-sized, whiskered head poked out from the yellow folds and dark, curious eyes peered out. Harry's five children squealed in delight, especially his seven-year-old daughter, Toni. The seal was dubbed "Andre" and was safely ensconced in the Goodridge's cellar, where he used a discarded bathtub for a playpen.

Soon Andre lived a double life: a Goodridge family member, sliding around the house or catnapping on the floor, and a harbor seal swimming and frolicking in Rockport Harbor.

Harry built a waterfront pen for Andre, and people began coming to watch Harry feed Andre. The young seal soon enjoyed the attention of the crowds. Andre mastered more than fifty commands and could put on quite an act, drawing an estimated 7,500 people during the summer of 1964.

The New England Aquarium in Boston offered to give Andre a warmer place to spend his winters, and it worked perfectly. Andre spent most of his winters there, delighting visitors from all parts of the country. Each spring they would take Andre to the shore and release him. The first year, no one knew if Andre would return to Rockport or go back to the wild, but year after year, Andre made the 150-plus-mile swim from Massachusetts back to his adoptive Rockport family. During the 1970s Andre's annual swim became a familiar spring ritual. Newspapers all over Maine and New England reported each Andre sighting as he made his way up the coast.

While Andre was becoming a celebrity, a young Joe Brennan quietly graduated from Boston College, earned his law degree and, in 1964, was elected to the first of three terms in Maine's House of Representatives. In the 1970s Brennan served in the Maine Senate, ran unsuccessfully to become the Democratic candidate for governor, and was elected to two terms as state attorney general. Having gained both experience and recognition, Brennan won the 1978 Democratic nomination and was elected governor. Filled with optimism, Joe Brennan was ready to take center stage and promote the programs on which he had based his campaign.

In the three months after his January 1979 inauguration, Governor Brennan became frustrated. Time after time, his proposals were practically ignored by the press. Preparing a speech for the April meeting of the Maine Press Association, Brennan decided to challenge their approach to news coverage. Articles speculating when Andre would make his spring return to Rockport had already begun appearing on Maine front pages. News about Brennan's proposals for court reform and other serious issues were relegated to pages deep inside the paper. Brennan chose the Andre headlines as an example of what was wrong. Brennan faced a room full of reporters, editors, and executives from the state's leading newspapers. Criticized for his low-key approach to leadership, he argued that it was the responsibility of the media to cover substantive issues, exciting or not:

> There should always be a place on the front page for the interesting, bright, human interest story. But in the end, it won't affect the progress of our state government, it won't change your local property tax rate, or the quality of your local fire department one bit if Andre reaches Rockport.

"Brennan on Press: Just Too Much Andre" read the *Portland Press Herald*'s headline the next morning. People all across Maine thought it was an unfair attack on their beloved Andre and responded angrily. Letters demanding an apology flooded the governor's office. Brennan had unleashed a firestorm, and the backlash of that comment would follow him for years.

The next month, when Andre actually began his annual swim back to Rockport, reporters couldn't resist ribbing the governor about coverage of Andre's pilgrimage. To the amusement of reporters, Brennan admitted that there was a "soft spot" in his heart for Andre. In an attempt to get back on track, he told them, "I would not want the remarks that I made recently to be misinterpreted as meaning you shouldn't cover his trip." Brennan talked of visiting Andre and referred to him as "Maine's most notable summer visitor." But, taking a cue from Andre, the people of Maine continued to give Governor Brennan what Portland papers called "the back of the flipper."

Reporters couldn't conceal their delight as the story kept getting better. Speaking to the Maine State Society in

Washington, D.C., Brennan admitted, "When I said the press made too much of Andre, it was construed as criticism of Andre. It was the worst thing I've done since I've been governor." Trying to defuse things with a bit of humor, Brennan joked that he now only read out-of-state papers because he didn't like to read negative stories about himself. He quipped, "Actually the [*Boston*] *Globe* sent a reporter to interview Andre, who said I was all wet and in over my head."

Brennan was not the first politician to realize Andre's influence with voters. Seeing Andre's popularity while visiting Maine back in 1964, twice-defeated presidential candidate Adlai Stevenson had laughingly suggested that perhaps the Republicans should nominate Andre to head their presidential ticket. Now Brennan agreed about Andre's political clout, remarking tongue in cheek, "It's clear that if Andre decided to run against me, he'd win."

On October 5, the Camden-Rockport Chamber of Commerce recognized Andre and Harry Goodridge for the international awareness they brought the area. A leather collar bearing a large medallion was placed around Andre's neck as he and Harry were named joint "Townspersons of the Year." Governor Brennan was not able to attend but, still trying to make amends, sent a telegram:

> Congratulations Andre, for too long you have not received the recognition you deserve. I think I am in a position to tell you that you have more fans and supporters than you know, believe me, because I have heard from all of them. I hope you do decide to become a full-time, year-round Maine resident. Maybe I can show you around Portland sometime.

Apparently, Andre was not willing to forgive. Right on cue Andre hissed loudly into the microphone during the telegram's reading—his only response to the governor. The press was more than willing to entertain its readers by extending the publicity catastrophe.

A year later, Andre served as ring bearer for the wedding of Harry's daughter, Toni Goodridge. Andre leaped through the harbor water to join them on a float at the Rockport Marine Park. At the appointed time he slid into the water, disappeared, and moments later popped out again clutching a small purse in his mouth. After delivering the purse containing the rings, Andre remained on the float while cameras flashed and whirred. Once again Andre was front page news in the Maine papers and, thanks to a television news crew from Washington, D.C., all over the country. Governor Brennan did not comment on the coverage.

As Brennan approached his 1982 re-election campaign, he decided it was time to patch things up with Andre. He gave the press an official comment. "I consider Andre a supporter. And I found out that if you don't give Andre his just priority, it will come home to get you."

Accordingly, Brennan arranged a trip to Andre's Rockport Harbor home. Brennan went out onto the wooden float over Andre's underwater pen. Harry Goodridge called Andre out of the water and acted as mediator, introducing Brennan to Andre. Photographers captured the meeting as governor visited seal. While Goodridge did not reveal all the details, he did report that Andre gave Brennan one of his trademark Bronx cheers. Maine newspapers covered the peace conference. "Andre harbored no bad feelings," Brennan told reporters. "I may have sealed the election right here."

Newspapers all over Maine covered the May 25 meeting between Andre and the governor. The three-year rivalry was over, and in the end Andre was not the only one to "forgive" the governor. Maine people apparently did too. That fall Governor Joseph E. Brennan was re-elected—in the process becoming the first Democrat since the Civil War to win every single county in the state of Maine.

On July 20, 1986, the *Maine Sunday Telegram* reported the death of Andre. People all over the state mourned the twenty-five-year-old seal. The *Portland Press Herald* remembered Andre with a touching editorial:

Who was abandoned by his mother, grew to become Maine's best known overweight bachelor, had a country-and-western song written about him and gave the Bronx cheer to Gov. Brennan? [Andre was] a bona fide celebrity . . . one of the few Mainers who was widely known simply by his first name. He was a rogue, a playboy, a carouser and a showoff. He was also Maine's official diplomat, its unelected governor, its most famous spokesperson, as highly regarded a native son as ever there was.

And a Child Shall Lead

·1983·

In the opening words of her book, *Journey to the Soviet Union*, Samantha Smith explained how she came into the world spotlight when she was only ten years old:

> Actually the whole thing started when I asked my mother if there was going to be a war . . . I woke up one morning and wondered if this was going to be the last day of the Earth. I asked my mother who would start a war and why.

In 1983 America was very concerned about the threat of attack by Soviet missiles. Samantha watched a scientist on public television explain the devastating effects of nuclear war. She was worried and confused.

Arthur and Jane Smith always encouraged their daughter to ask questions and to look for answers. Jane showed Samantha a news article about Yuri Andropov's recent election as General Secretary of the Communist Party, head of the Soviet Union. They read it together and talked. No one Samantha knew wanted war, and the article didn't sound like the Soviet people did either. Why would two countries who claimed not to want war continue to build enough nuclear missiles and weapons to destroy the world many times over?

Samantha thought maybe the leaders wanted war. She asked her mother to write Andropov a letter "to find out who was causing all the trouble." Jane said, "Why don't *you* write to him?" When she was five, Samantha had written the Queen of England and had received an answer from a lady-in-waiting. Why not write Andropov? Using what she later called her "most careful handwriting," Samantha wrote the new Soviet leader with the candid directness of a child:

Dear Mr. Andropov,

My name is Samantha Smith. I am ten years old. Congratulations on your new job. I have been worrying about Russia and the United States getting into a nuclear war. Are you going to vote to have a war or not? If you aren't please tell me how you are going to help to not have a war. This question you do not have to answer, but I would like to know why you want to conquer the world or at least our country. God made the world for us to live together in peace and not to fight.

Sincerely,

Samantha Smith

Samantha's mother helped her address the envelope to the Kremlin, Moscow, USSR. Her dad checked the postage, 40 cents, and mailed the letter.

That winter Samantha continued her normal routines. She went to class at Manchester Elementary School and played with friends. She loved playing in the snow and was always ready for a good snowball fight. When it was too cold, Samantha would curl up with a favorite mystery or animal book.

Samantha had almost forgotten about her letter when she

was called to the school office in April for a phone call. A reporter for United Press International wanted to talk to her. He told Samantha about an article in *Pravda,* the official Russian newspaper. The article included a picture of a letter to Andropov. Had Samantha really written a letter about war to Andropov? Samantha knew nothing about a *Pravda* article, but said yes, she wrote a letter, and no, she had not received an answer.

Samantha's father had the article translated. Samantha was disappointed; it neither answered her question nor said why Andropov hadn't replied. She wrote again, this time to the Soviet Embassy in Washington, D.C. She asked that Andropov please answer her questions, explaining later, "I thought my questions were good ones and it shouldn't matter if I was ten years old."

On Monday, April 25, 1983, the amazing happened. The spunky eleven-year-old girl from Manchester, Maine, received a letter from the General Secretary of the Union of Soviet Socialist Republics. Samantha had received her answer on two and a half neatly typed pages. Andropov compared Samantha to Becky Thatcher in *Tom Sawyer.* He tried to explain why countries wage war and repeatedly assured her the Soviet people wanted peace. He invited Samantha to come to the Soviet Union that summer to see firsthand that the Soviet people also wanted "peace and friendship among peoples."

Once the story of Samantha's letter hit the news media, life at the Smith house was a blur of visitors and interviews. Reporters from *People, Time, Newsweek,* public radio, and NBC-TV squeezed lights and sound equipment between the living room furniture or around the kitchen table as they took turns interviewing Samantha. Then Samantha was flown to New York for the *Today* show. That Friday, just four days after the letter arrived, Samantha flew to California and appeared live on the *Tonight Show,* talking and giggling with Johnny Carson. Everything was happening so fast.

When the Smiths returned from California, downtown Manchester looked different. Store windows were decorated with Samantha's pictures, posters, and congratulatory signs. She was a hometown hero, and the brunette with the dancing blue eyes quickly became America's sweetheart.

America was not the only place captivated by Samantha's heart, quick grin, and personality. Representatives from the Soviet press eagerly interviewed Samantha. Plans began for the Smiths to visit the Soviet Union in July. The next ten weeks were a flurry of activity. They juggled work, school, travel arrangements, interviews, and packing. Samantha wanted gifts for the children and dignitaries she would meet. Her room filled with decals, postcards, key rings, tie tacks, and T-shirts—anything with Maine insignias. With the last suitcase packed, the Smiths left on July 7, accompanied by local reporters. During the next two weeks, Samantha won the hearts of the Soviet people.

Returning to the Augusta airport on July 22, Samantha was welcomed back by a crowd of reporters, neighbors, and friends. The change in Samantha was remarkable. Earlier interviews showed a girl, all arms, legs, and giggles. Now Samantha faced reporters with composure, calm and confident as she fielded each question.

Some things had not changed. Her mother still insisted that homework be done before television. Samantha was delighted that her friends at Maranacook Community School didn't treat her like a celebrity. She was happier going to a school dance than meeting a "big shot in Washington," according to her mother. But Samantha was a celebrity, and the media did not want to let the girl from Manchester, Maine, go back to anonymity. Samantha was a symbol for all the children of the world who wanted peace. Samantha spoke at the Children's International Symposium in Kobe, Japan. She hosted a Disney Channel special on politics, elections, and government during the 1984 presidential campaign. Everywhere Samantha went, people wanted to hear about the Soviet Union.

At home in Manchester, Samantha wrote *Journey to the Soviet Union* to share her trip. Filled with pictures and telling her story, it was published in August 1984. In the foreword, Dr. Lee Salk of Rockwood, Maine, a leader in the KidsPeace national organization, summed up the impact of Samantha's year and a half in the public eye:

> Samantha Smith has become a symbol of hope to all children. Her simple question, supported by loving parents, led to greater human understanding, and has shown us the power of a child in lessening the tensions between two world powers.

Samantha moved from celebrated peace advocate to popular celebrity status when she was hired as an actress in *Lime Street,* a television series starring Robert Wagner. Samantha's father, a professor, took a leave of absence and went to California with her as Samantha pursued acting with the same energy she had pursued an answer to her question.

In August 1985 Samantha and her dad were returning from *Lime Street* filming in London. The last leg of the trip was on a commuter plane. Jane Smith waited eagerly at the Augusta airport. It was a stormy Sunday night and the plane was diverted to the small Auburn–Lewiston Municipal Airport. At 10:12 P.M. the plane crashed and burned in the woods off Foster Road, just short of the airport. Samantha and Arthur Smith, along with the crew and six other passengers, were all killed instantly.

Just as people around the world had embraced Samantha's youthful charm and exuberance, now they were stunned by the news of her death. All three Soviet media organizations covered the story, unheard of for an American. Her funeral, televised live in Maine, was transmitted by satellite to the Soviet Union. At the funeral Soviet spokesman Vladimir Kulagin said,

"Samantha was like a small but very powerful and brilliant beam of sunshine which penetrated the thunderstorm clouds." The Soviets issued a stamp honoring Samantha and named a mountain, diamond, flower, and even a planet for her.

Elementary students in Bethel, Maine, wrote essays on "What Samantha Smith Meant to Me" and gave the collection to Samantha's mother. A Samantha Smith Foundation was formed with contributions from all corners of the United States. Those contributions enabled the foundation to sponsor youth exchanges from 1985 to 1995. Maine schoolchildren sent money toward a memorial statue. In front of the Maine State Museum, the completed life-size statue depicts Samantha releasing a dove of peace, while a bear cub, symbol of both Maine and Russia, sits at her feet.

Samantha Smith remains frozen in time as a young girl, filled with a child's hope and idealism. Only thirteen when she died, Samantha found rock concerts too loud and could barely imagine getting her driver's license. But according to her mother, Samantha never stopped dreaming of world peace. As Samantha put it:

> Sometimes I still worry that the next day will be the
> last day of the Earth, but with more people thinking
> about the problems of the world, I hope that some-
> day soon we will find the way to world peace.
> Maybe someone will show us the way.

Samantha led the way. Her simple questions, engaging smile, and determination to spread hope were all a model for breaking down barriers between people. President Reagan and General Secretary Andropov have been replaced. The Soviet Union is no longer. More countries have nuclear capability, and there are new methods of mass destruction. The players and weapons change, but the problem remains. Samantha's dream of peace and an end to war is as relevant today as it was in 1983.

Progress on the Line
· 1983 ·

Driving through Bryant Pond, Maine, in January of 1981, you might not have thought it unique. In the mountains near the New Hampshire border, the village of Bryant Pond is part of the town of Woodstock. The village has about 800 people, most living in mill houses along Route 26. You might have passed the general store and stopped to eat at Jochem Robiller's restaurant. If that was all, you might have left Bryant Pond unaware. But if you had asked for a pay phone, you would quickly have spotted something different. You might have been surprised, perhaps even momentarily offended, if the waitress asked if you wanted to make a crank call. For at the pay phone in Robiller's restaurant, or for that matter, any phone in Bryant Pond, all you could make was crank calls.

All 450 phones in the Bryant Pond Telephone Company system were hand-crank phones. The antique magneto system was the last of its kind operating in the United States, a living museum to communication history. Towns all across the nation were switching from what they considered old-fashioned dial phones to modern push-button pulse phones. Bryant Pond still used truly old-fashioned wire-and-plug switchboards.

Almost thirty years earlier, Elden Hathaway had been worried about job cuts at his mill when he heard that the local phone company was for sale. Having worked a magneto-powered switchboard in his youth in Michigan, Hathaway decided to take the chance. When he bought it, there were only one hundred customers, three full-time operators, one full-time lineman, and three part-time employees. Now there were 450 customers, hundreds of miles of wire, and ten full-time and part-time employees. The two wood frame switchboards still operated out of the living room of Hathaway's Rumford Avenue home.

The hand-cranked magneto phone system developed around the turn of the century. When an operator would turn her crank, a magneto in the crank would generate a ringing current, which would travel the wire and make a dial at the customer's phone ring. In the base of the customer's phone, a large battery supplied the talking power after the call had been connected.

When Hathaway purchased the phone company, each Bryant Pond Company customer had a wooden box mounted on a wall. On the front of the box were two shiny bells and on the side a small metal crank. A cord connected the box to a freestanding, black cup mouthpiece. Another cord was attached to a cylindrical cone earpiece that hung from a hook next to the mouthpiece when not in use. To make a call a customer wound the crank. The operator at the Hathaway's house got the signal on the antique switchboard and made a connection by plugging one of her many wires into the plug for that specific phone. To call someone without going through the operator, a customer would crank the designated combination of short and long rings. By 1981 most of the wall boxes had been replaced by tabletop crank boxes that connected to a more traditional-style black phone receiver with speaker and microphone combination handset.

Many townspeople felt a pride in the old phone system. Comparing it to San Francisco's cable cars, they enjoyed being unique. Alice Johnson, president of the local League of Women Voters, recognized the tourist appeal: "Let's face it, aside from our beautiful lake and lovely neighborhood, we don't have much else. The crank telephone is what puts this town on the map. Anything that can get tourists into central Maine, away from the lobster pots, is important."

In 1973 they had come close to losing their crank phones. Two local realtors had been frustrated by the difficulty Bell Telephone operators sometimes had with the Bryant Pond system and they appealed to the Maine Public Utilities Commission (PUC) to require the system be modernized. The PUC scheduled public meetings, held at the elementary school, and over 200 residents showed up to speak for keeping the old phones. Everyone had a story of a time when the operators and the old system had made a difference.

Between the lights on the switchboard and local operators who could recognize customer voices, there were many stories of potential disasters averted: the youngster who just rang up the operator and yelled "Fire!" and hung up without saying who or where; the sick woman who was only able to say, "I need help"; the three-year-old who just kept saying his mother had fallen off the roof. In each case the operator knew the exact phone location and was able to send help immediately. Harold Tyler, fire chief for twenty-three years, said, "The hand-crank telephone company has saved lives and property." Many times the operator would reach him away from home to tell him of a fire, then she would call the rest of the department while he got started. No one needed an answering machine; the operator would take a message for people when they weren't home, and she would reroute calls to you if you let her know where you were going.

But the personal service Hathaway gave went beyond emergencies, beyond phone service. One night a young girl became nervous when she thought she heard strange noises while babysitting. She called the operator to report the sounds. When Hathaway heard, he drove out to the girl's house and stayed with her until everything was checked out and the girl felt comfortable.

As Patricia Early said, "The hand-crank way allows a lot of

personal caring about people to come through." Hathaway agreed. "They like the feeling that a helping hand is just a crank away. When they leave town, they have a built-in answering service, or if they are in a hurry and can't reach a number, we'll keep trying for them and call them back when the line is free. These are things they would miss with a dial system."

Bryant Pond won. The PUC ruled the town did *not* have to modernize its phone system and that the problem was with Bell System employees, not the crank system. The PUC agreed with the residents that there were advantages to the older system, "especially when placed into perspective with the increasing depersonalization and indifference which is an unfortunate by-product of modern life."

Progress will not wait forever and time does not stand still. People and their opinions change. In 1981, sixty-three-year-old Hathaway was ready to retire. After much thought and lengthy negotiations, he sold the Bryant Pond Telephone Company to Oxford County Telephone and Telegraph in July. A month after the sale, Oxford announced a plan to replace the crank phones with a modern dial-tone system over two years.

Townspeople Brad Hooper and Alice Johnson quickly formed a committee and appealed to the PUC to be able to keep the old crank system. Dubbing their campaign "Don't Yank the Crank," they started a public relations blitz. They collected more than one thousand signatures from residents and people all over the state urging the PUC to order the Oxford company to let them keep the historic and neighborly form of service. ABC-TV's *Good Morning, America* did a feature on Bryant Pond, and the committee began receiving orders for "Don't Yank the Crank" T-shirts from all over the country. The news spread. Soon calls and letters poured in offering help to save the crank system.

This time the PUC hearings were very different. People still shared moving stories of how the crank system's human touch had made a difference, but the overall mood had shifted.

When the PUC announced its official denial on November 24, 1982, lawyer John Feehan, representing Oxford, conceded that the crank system was the last in the United States and had a "certain sentimental value. . . . There are now better methods of bringing telecommunication services to the public [however]." There was some talk of trying to appeal the decisions to allow individual customers the right to choose between the modern dial system or the old crank, but the final decision was not to appeal. Progress had beaten tradition. The need for a speedy, complex communication system had won over the historical and emotional value of more personal service.

The conversion cost over $300,000 and took until the fall of 1983. At the home of one family after another, the crank phones sat next to new dial phones awaiting final connection. Some longtime customers were allowed to purchase their wooden crank box phones for $3.00 each. Bryant Pond was again in local and national news as the days counted down.

On October 11 the days finally ran out. The American Legion Hall was readied for Oxford's celebration party. Hooper's general store, unofficial "Don't Yank the Crank" headquarters, prepared for a more quiet marking of an era's passing. Officials and family gathered in Elden Hathaway's living room. Television crews, reporters, and locals formed a crowd outside the house.

At 2:12 P.M. Hathaway looked on as the last call was connected and pulled the wire from the plug when the call ended. Oxford's manager, F. Robert Jamison, flipped a switch and pulled a heat coil, shutting down the antique system. Bryant Pond was now in direct contact with phone subscribers all over the world. Beneath the headline "Bryant Pond Joins Direct-Dial World," reporters wrote that "sparks flew and cameras flashed [as] Bryant Pond lost its biggest claim to fame."

Elden Hathaway once tried to explain the essence of the Bryant Pond Telephone Company:

We have helped babies get born, fires get put out, and doctors get to people who needed them. And we have done a lot of things that were just plain fun to do. Like talking to a small boy the first time he ever used the phone or calling someone with news of [a] new baby. These are all the things you can't put a dollar value on.

Phone companies have found ways to automate, name, and price some of the services Bryant Pond operators provided daily. Families can pay extra for call forwarding, call waiting, conference calls, and voice mail. Communities spend thousands for the safety features of Enhanced 911. But in a day of prerecorded instructions, computerized transfers, and mechanical voices, one intangible remains lost. The sense of community and human contact with the familiar voice of a local, human operator has yet to be duplicated.

Justice Delayed

· 2002 ·

Lorraine Luttrell looked out over the water from the deck of the Coast Guard ship. It was a clear fall day as they headed to a point southeast of Cape Elizabeth. A few more miles and she could fulfill the promise to her husband John. Fifty years earlier John had watched his ship go down at that spot. He had been nineteen years old.

The Casco Bay waters were choppy, but men on the deck of the USS *Eagle* could see beyond the other ships far into the distance. The clear April skies made it a great day for aerial target practice. Below deck men carried out routine tasks as the patrol boat towed the target out of Portland Harbor.

The 200-foot *Eagle* (designated PE-56) was part of the extensive U.S. Navy presence in 1945 Portland. Portland's shipyard turned out 274 ships during World War II, and because its deepwater harbor was the closest to Europe, the harbor was always busy. During a single week the previous August, 588 ships had departed and entered Portland Harbor. Used as a summer training vessel for reservists before the United States entered the war, the *Eagle* was a familiar sight in Portland.

Having deployed the target, the *Eagle* came to a stop, dead in the water. John Luttrell, who had been on deck watch, left the bridge shortly after 12:05 P.M. Suddenly, at 12:14 P.M. on April 23, 1945, a 300-foot water geyser shot straight into the air. The *Eagle* exploded, broke in half, and immediately began to sink. The blast was seen by those on the nearby destroyer *Selfridge,* people on shore, and at Portland Head's lighthouse.

Joseph Priestas thought it felt like the *Eagle* had hit a floating mine or had been hit by a really close depth charge. Lieutenant J. G. John Scagnelli remembers: "[A] terrific explosion knocked me out of bed and against a bulkhead. I was thrown just as if someone had picked me up and tossed me. [The passageway was] filled with smoke, low pressure steam, and debris." By the time Scagnelli climbed a ladder to the main deck and passed the starboard galley, he was in water up to his chest, then out in the open water. He later estimated that as little as forty seconds had passed since the explosion.

John Breeze had been working a crossword puzzle with a fellow crewman when the ship exploded. The ship immediately listed, and with water rising, he looked for a life jacket. Oscar Davis saw that the explosion had blown off the closest ladder to the deck. Wading through water and twisted metal, he followed Breeze, trying to remain calm. They joined the group frantically trying to get topside. Ahead of Davis and Breeze was John Luttrell. Breeze, much larger than Luttrell, reached up and "raised [Luttrell] five steps with one push on the behind." Finally up and off the ship, they swam, searching for something to buoy them in the water.

William Thompson was blown through a hatch, losing a sock and shoe before he landed in the water. Second Class Machinist's Mate Harold Peterson was below deck in an aft bunk compartment when the blast shook the whole ship. Thrown into a metal locker and hit by an overturned bunk, he recovered and headed topside. Assisting an injured sailor, Peterson encouraged others to get into the water and away from the ship. "It seemed like an explosion on the starboard side, and in fifteen seconds I was on deck and water was up to my ankles," he testified later. Cletus Frane jumped over the side with Daniel Jaronik. Frane was being pulled under by the suction of the sinking ship when an empty wooden Coke case hit him in the shoulder and he was able to grab onto it. Jaronik grabbed part of the target buoy. Radioman Third Class John Wisniewski was the last person out of his compartment to make it up and into the water.

The aft section disappeared first. Then the forward section sank and the *Eagle* was gone. Scagnelli joined Luttrell and Breeze holding a floating metal oil tank until it sank. Peterson grabbed a floating piece of wood and swam it to Scagnelli, Luttrell, and Breeze. Clutching anything that would float, a scattering of sailors struggled to stay afloat until rescue came.

The destroyer *Selfridge* was there in minutes, but minutes can be too long when hypothermia sets in. Unable to hang on, several who survived the explosion drowned in the bone-chilling, forty-degree water. The last survivor was picked up by 12:31, only seventeen minutes after the explosion.

Thirteen men were rescued by the destroyer USS *Selfridge*. Treated at a Portland hospital, mostly for minor cuts and bruises, all but two were released quickly. Only two bodies were recovered. Scagnelli later told authorities he believed at least twenty men had been trapped in quarters below deck. A single empty life jacket, a few empty oil barrels, pieces of timber, and bits of general debris were all that was left of the *Eagle*. Forty-nine men had died.

Despite the enormity of the disaster and the fact that the explosion was seen by people along the shore, Portland newspapers that night did not even acknowledge the explosion. Nor did they the next day, or the next. The country was at war and the press was tightly censored. Sixteen days later, on May 9, a headline stretched across the top of the Portland papers: "49 Die in Mysterious Boat Blast Three Miles off Cape Elizabeth." Below it was a subhead: "Stalin Announces Surrender of Germany." The families of the forty-nine men had already received telegrams, notifying that each had been "lost at sea." The only explanation given was a boiler explosion.

The official court of inquiry met and heard testimony from

the survivors and witnesses. A U-boat sighting was reported in the area just before the sinking. The boiler had been over-hauled and checked just two weeks earlier. A navy destroyer picked up a sonar target but found nothing. Depth charges were ordered and dropped into the night, with no apparent results. Five of the survivors reported seeing glimpses of a U-boat, exhaust, or conning tower just after the explosion. Some even described the red-and-yellow markings of a trotting horse on a shield, painted on the tower as it became a silhouette and disappeared. Survivor John Breeze said: "I only saw it momen-tarily. You don't think about things like that. All you think about is saving your own life."

Although the court thought the blast might have been an enemy mine or an enemy torpedo, the inquiry concluded in its official verdict that the blast "was the result of a boiler explo-sion, the cause of which could not be determined." Scagnelli, the only surviving officer, wrote letters to each family, but he was ordered to say that it was a boiler explosion and not to mention any suspicion of a U-boat.

Nineteen-year-old John Luttrell settled in a small house in South Portland after the war. He was always angry that the navy labeled the sinking an "accident." He knew what he had seen. He knew what his shipmates testified they had seen. Yet the navy stood by its ruling. Twenty years later, Luttrell told his second wife, Lorraine, "We all *knew* it was a U-boat." She remembers, "It used to upset [him] terribly." In addition, because it was labeled an accident rather than act of war, the men were denied recognition for their bravery and loss. There are no medals given for accidents. As the years passed, Luttrell spoke less and less about the day the *Eagle* sank.

When Luttrell died in 1996, his last instructions showed he had never forgotten the attack. Lorraine was carrying out his final request on that fall day. The ship came to a stop and two Coast Guardsmen joined her. Neither of them looked much older than John had been in 1945. One stood at attention with a crisp salute, while the other leaned carefully over the side. Lorraine watched as John Luttrell's ashes drifted slowly onto the water, floating for a bit before settling beneath the surface. No fancy funeral. No speeches. No flag-draped coffin. After fifty-one years John Luttrell was finally reunited with his *Eagle* shipmates.

The truth about the PE-56 came out in 2002, five years after Luttrell's death. Three sons of *Eagle* victim Ivar Westerlund became friends with Paul Lawton, a lawyer who was a military historian and was fascinated by submarines. Hearing the story of the *Eagle* one night in March 1998, he began a quest to find the truth. He spent years investigating declassified German and American documents and testimony. The case was reopened. After carefully studying the evidence, Bernard Cavalcante, senior archivist at the Naval Historical Center in Washington, D. C., sent detailed documentation to Secretary of the Navy Gordon England, in May 2001. Included was a letter formally recommending that the record be changed.

The record was officially changed and the facts were finally made public. The *Eagle* was sunk by a torpedo from the German submarine U-583, commanded by Helmut von Fromsdorf. The U-583 was sunk off Rhode Island just twelve days later—four days before news of the *Eagle*'s explosion appeared in the Portland headline.

In June 2002 a ceremony was held honoring the *Eagle* and its men. Purple Hearts were given first to the three surviving men of the USS *Eagle*. Then the rest of the crew's names were read as their families were presented with their medals. The day was long overdue. After fifty-seven years the courage and sacrifice of the men of the USS *Eagle* were recognized and celebrated at last.

Seeds for a Miracle
· 2003 ·

Seeds of Peace Camp Director Tim Wilson gently rang the bell and watched for signs of life in the cabins along the lake. Usually, he rang it loudly and vigorously to rouse the campers at 7:30 to start another day. This morning, it was muted and rang at 6:40. Campers began to get out of bed.

The Quaker meeting had been announced at dinner the night before. The camp regularly held open services for a wide range of religions. This morning's Quaker silent meeting would be another new experience. Today the campers would start the day remembering why this camp was different. They were here to replace hatred, stereotypes, and ignorance with human relationships. In 1997 Kofi Annan, secretary-general of the United Nations, had described the nonsectarian, nonpartisan camp as "bringing together young people who have seen the ravages of war to learn the art of peace." The meeting was to focus on that goal and to honor the people who had lost their lives in conflicts around the world.

Bobbie Gottschalk walked toward the main hall where she would begin the meeting. The lake was a mirror, silent and still, so early in the morning. Exact images of the docks and boats were reflected in the unbroken water. Fog shrouded the tops of the trees, and in spots a mist rose from the lake. The camp seemed suspended in time and space.

Campers walked from their cabins in small groups, quiet and thoughtful, with none of the usual morning hubbub. The first to enter the hall silently filled the large ring of benches. As more arrived they sat on the floor inside the ring. No one could be left outside the circle.

Soon Bobbie was surrounded by over one hundred campers, most of whom had traveled halfway around the world to come to Otisfield, Maine. They were Israeli, Jordanian, American, and Palestinian. Examples of the best and brightest, the teenagers had been chosen by their countries because of their potential to become leaders. Camp was emotionally and psychologically challenging, but it needed to be. They were here to learn the skills and develop the strength to change the world. They were here to become the seeds of peace.

When everyone had gathered, Bobbie explained that Quakers believe everyone has a God-given goodness within. They believe you must sit in community and strip yourself of daily concerns. In the silence you search to find that inner goodness, and only then you speak what is in your heart. Everyone is equal and first names are the rule.

Bobbie began as she had every year for three years, reading from the writings of Asel Asleh, a former camper. She included his favorite quote from the thirteenth-century writer Mevlana Jalal e-Din Rumi: "Out beyond ideas of wrong-doing and right-doing, there is a field. I'll meet you there." She continued with a promise Asel had written in a 1998 e-mail encouraging fellow campers:

> I will make this place a better place to live in and I
> will go on. For all the souls who only saw pain and
> sorrow in their eyes; for the souls who will never see
> the pain of another soul; I promise you I will go on.

Asel had been killed two years after writing those words, but each of those gathered had come to share the quest. Their dream was to make the world a better place, to stop the pain of violence and hatred, to learn respect and teach it to others.

The struggle was to continue against a world that seemed determined to cling to fear and distrust, to go on regardless of the obstacles.

Bobbie called for silence.

The silence enveloped the group as the fog surrounded the camp, isolating the building from its surroundings just as the camp isolated the campers from their past beliefs and experiences. In the silence the campers worked to rid themselves of more than daily concerns. They struggled to release the tradition and teaching of hatred, the assumptions of animosity. The silence was powerful, giving campers time to reflect. They thought about the atmosphere of fear, distrust, and war at home. They remembered the attitudes and fears they had brought with them, afraid even to sleep in the same cabin with their enemies. They considered what they had learned at the cultural nights, arts programs, and in the group challenges. They contemplated each small step and transformation they had experienced in the first two weeks of camp.

Out of the silence they began to speak.

One camper spoke of the man who began the Seeds of Peace quest. John Wallach had recently died, and the camp felt his absence. Another told how Wallach had watched the 1993 coverage of the first World Trade Center bombing and was inspired to take personal action aimed at changing the climate of the world. They recounted his vision of a camp for teens old enough to learn and young enough to change. He would bring them to neutral ground in Maine, where they would eat, work, and play side by side. In the process they would develop new beliefs and skills, slowly learning to see human faces instead of enemies. He made the vision a reality. Wallach's dream was that these teenagers would return to their homes and begin working to change attitudes. The camp would teach and nurture the teens to become the seeds of a more peaceful world.

A ninety-three-year-old camp volunteer rose to speak of Asel Asleh, whose words had opened the meeting. Asel had attended Seeds of Peace camp for three years and been a very active member of the ongoing Seeds community. A gifted writer, fluent in three languages, Asel was a pioneer of the Seeds of Peace online community, writing hundreds of e-mails encouraging fellow Seeds and traveling miles to visit as many as he could. An Israeli Arab, Asel was committed to the goals of Seeds of Peace; he owned thirty green Seeds of Peace T-shirts and wore them everywhere, always looking for opportunities to spread the message. But in October of 2000, the seventeen-year-old became a victim of the violence in the Middle East. The first and only Seeds of Peace camper to be killed, Asel was wearing a Seeds of Peace T-shirt the day he was killed. Even as his family grieved, they chose to have him buried in a Seeds shirt and to continue to honor his dreams.

The volunteer spoke at length, not only of Asel's gifts, but also of the quality of his family evident in Asel and in their reaction to Asel's death. He spoke of the fellow Seeds, Arabs and Israelis alike, welcomed in Asel's home, sharing grief for his loss. They remembered their son as "a pioneer of humanity and love" who "worked so hard to bring alive the human spirit."

Others who remembered Asel spoke of his ability to argue persuasively without being provocative. Some spoke of his broad shoulders and smiling face, but most of all, the heart that inspired everyone to share his dream.

One by one campers and staff spoke . . . no overlapping, no interruptions, each sensing when someone was through or another was ready to speak. Gradually, the words held less sadness and more hope. In the isolation of that room, the chance to believe in and create a new reality began to be heard.

Some remembered struggling with painful issues during coexistence sessions when, with the help of new friends, it suddenly seemed possible to change. A camper recalled learning "to erase all the prejudice in my head, and to look at the world through a pair of eyes that were unclouded with hatred and fear."

Campers spoke of needing to go on, even without Asel, without John—to go on *for* Asel, *for* John, for all the friends, and relatives, and unknown people whose lives had been lost in conflict, violence, and hatred around the world. The children of war pledged to become the tools to break the cycle of violence.

When there was a feeling that all had said what their hearts needed to say, the room was filled with the strength of the combined community. Bobbie knew that the campers would need this strength when they left the neutral world of the camp. When the last speaker was through, she let the silence of community warm the room for a few moments while each one absorbed the words that had been shared.

Bobbie quietly signaled Tim Wilson to ring the bell, a final soft tone to mark the end of the meeting. As the group left the hall and dispersed, many walked over to spend a few moments in the quiet meditation garden beside the hall.

In the garden are three granite benches. One is in memory of young Maine peace advocate Samantha Smith. The other two are placed in memory of John Wallach and of Asel Asleh, the founder and the Seed. They shared a dream of the miracle that would be possible when the teenage Seeds who began their journey together in the Maine woods might one day sit around a table as leaders of a new, more peaceful world. Neither lived to see the reality, but in the first ten years of Seeds of Peace, over 2,000 campers have come to share the dream.

This is just the beginning. Seeds of Peace Vice President Bobbie Gottschalk will continue to introduce campers to silent meetings. Campers will continue to explore each other's cultures. Counselors and facilitators at the camp will lead new campers to share the dream. John Wallach believed that the future of peace rested with the next generation. Asel Asleh accepted the challenge saying, "When we became Seeds we took in our hands a responsibility. It is our job now to do it the right way, no matter what." Seeds of Peace campers are scattered around the world. In twenty-two nations they, too, have accepted Wallach's challenge to build a more peaceful world. Like Asel, they work each day to "make this place a better place to live in." Like Asel, *for* Asel, they will go on.

A Potpourri of Maine Facts

- If you stretched Maine's jagged coastline straight, its 3,478 miles would reach farther than the distance from New York City, New York, to San Francisco, California.

- Eighty-seven percent of Mainers report having seen a moose; 13 percent saw the moose while looking out a window at home.

- Despite an average seasonal snowfall of 70.7 inches in Portland, southern Maine has a "brown" Christmas (no snow on the ground) almost 50 percent of the time.

- Maine has 6,000 lakes and ponds and 5,151 rivers and streams—the most of any state.

- Maine has more than 2,000 coastal islands.

- The highest point on the Atlantic Coast is Mount Desert Island's Cadillac Mountain at 1,530 feet.

- Maine's 5,268-foot Mount Katahdin is the northern end of the Appalachian Trail.

- Maine has a 92-mile wilderness waterway along the Allagash River in northern Maine.

- Trees cover 90 percent of Maine's land area.

• Maine's Aroostook County has a land area larger than that of Rhode Island and Connecticut combined—6,453 square miles.

• The average commute for Maine workers is nineteen minutes.

• Maine raises 98 percent of the low-bush blueberries in the United States.

• In 1717 notorious pirate "Black Sam" Bellamy planned his own kingdom, starting with a base of operations along the Machias River. Though no pirate gold has ever been found there, treasure hunters still poke along the river's tidal flats and try to see remnants of Bellamy's breastworks and moats in the ridges and hollows near where the bridge crosses the Machias River.

• The first lighthouse authorized by the federal government was Portland Head Light, in Cape Elizabeth, Maine. It is the oldest American lighthouse still in operation and widely reported to be the most photographed lighthouse in the world.

• Paul Revere was in charge of ordnances for nineteen ships and twenty-four transports attempting to recapture Castine, Maine, from the British in 1779. The largest naval operation of the American Revolution, it became the biggest U.S. naval disaster prior to Pearl Harbor and resulted in court-martial charges being filed against Revere.

• Established in 1794, the Shaker community at Sabbathday Lake in New Gloucester, Maine, is the last remaining active Shaker community in America.

• More than one hundred years before the founding of the United Nations, Maine pacifist William Ladd proposed a worldwide Congress of Nations in a dissertation written in 1831, while serving as the first president of the American Peace Society.

• Mary Baker Eddy, who later founded Christian Science, first experienced the use of willpower and personal magnetism for healing in Portland, Maine. She was being treated in October 1862 at the office of Dr. Phineas P. Quimby.

• The largest wooden vessel ever constructed, the six-masted cargo schooner *Wyoming,* was built in Bath, Maine, in 1909. Today's missile frigates are 3,400–3,600 tons. The *Wyoming* weighed a whopping 3,730 tons and could carry more than 6,000 tons of cargo.

• Maine's governor Percival Baxter tried to persuade the state legislature to purchase Maine's largest mountain, Mount Katahdin. When unsuccessful, Baxter bought it himself. He bought land, parcel by parcel, and starting in 1931, he eventually donated a total of 200,000 acres as a personal gift to the people of Maine. The only condition was that it be preserved forever as a wilderness area. Now named Baxter State Park, up to 73,000 people visit each summer, and as many as 889 per month camp there in the winter.

• Kittery, Maine, could be considered the birthplace of the United States submarine fleet. The first submarine built by the navy (1917), the first navy-built atomic submarine (USS *Swordfish*), and the first Polaris sub (USS *Lincoln*) were all built there.

• The nation's longest continuous religious broadcast began in 1926 on Portland's WCSH radio. The First Radio Parish Church of America began under the Reverend Howard Hough and continues today on WCSH-TV under its fifth pastor, the Reverend Peter Pantagore.

• After serving four terms in the House of Representatives, Margaret Chase Smith of Skowhegan became the first woman elected to both houses of Congress, when she was elected to the U.S. Senate in 1948. Refusing to be intimidated during the McCarthy Era, she took the Congress to task fewer than six months later. Her "Declaration of Conscience" speech condemned the bigotry of McCarthy's tactics and demonstrated Smith's courage and her dedication to the American ideals of justice.

• Maine is the only state which has repeatedly elected independent governors: James B. Longley in 1975 and Angus S. King, Jr., in 1995 and 1999.

• Maine consistently has one of the lowest crime rates in the nation. In 2002 there were only fourteen murders in the entire state, $\frac{1}{1000}$ the national total. Maine ranks forty-ninth in the nation for violent crimes per 100,000 people.

• Maine's largest city, Portland, has surprising cultural diversity. At Portland High School there are fifty-two different native languages spoken.

A Medley of Maine "Firsts"

1623—First sawmill in America (on the Piscataqua River near what soon became York, Maine).

1625—The first road pavement in America is laid in Pemaquid, Maine. It is made of rocks, stones, and cobblestones and is 33 feet wide.

1642—York, Maine, becomes America's first officially chartered town on March 1.

1705—Father Sebastian Rasle builds the first native school in Norridgewock, Maine, and compiles an extensive dictionary of the Abenaki language. Containing over 7,500 words, plus notes on grammar and usage, it is at Harvard University today.

1851—The "Maine Law" is the first law in the United States outlawing the sale of alcoholic beverages. It forbade all sales except those for "medicinal" and "industrial" uses.

1872—J. F. Blondel of Thomaston, Maine, patents the first doughnut cutter on July 9.

1875—The first African-American bishop in America,

James A. Healy, is named to the Portland, Maine, diocese. During his twenty-five-year tenure, the diocese built sixty churches, eighteen schools, eighteen convents, and numerous welfare institutions. These were needed to serve the Catholic population of the state, which had doubled in that same time.

1877—First earmuffs are patented March 13, by thirteen-year-old Chester Greenwood, of Farmington, Maine.

1900—Mrs. Maynard Hanson of Portland, Maine, becomes the first woman automobile driver licensed.

1912—First Camp Fire Girls Organization is announced at Sebago Lake, Maine, on March 17.

1962—The first transoceanic television program was telecast July 10 via the Telstar communications satellite, whose ground station was in Andover, Maine. This live transmission ushered in the age of global communications.

1977—Maine was the first state to adopt a law prohibiting forced retirement at age sixty-five.

1980—The Maine Indian Land Claims Settlement Agreement is the largest of its kind and the first to include provisions for reacquiring land. A key factor in the legal basis for the claim was a copy of a 1794 treaty, found in a shoe box of old documents in a Passamaquoddy home in 1957.

2002—Maine becomes the first state to provide laptop computers for students statewide. The Maine Learning Technology Initiative put Apple iBooks in the hands of every seventh-grade student in the state. By 2003 the program included all seventh- and eighth-graders, and plans were being explored to expand the program into high schools.

Bibliography

History

Agger, Lee. *Women of Maine*. Portland, ME: Guy Gannett Publishing, 1982.

Bourque, Bruce J. *Twelve Thousand Years: American Indians in Maine*. Lincoln: University of Nebraska Press, 2001.

Caldwell, Bill. *Lighthouses of Maine*. Portland, ME: Gannett Books, 1986.

———. *Rivers of Fortune: Where Maine Tides and Money Flowed*. Portland, ME: Guy Gannett Publishing, 1983.

Cowan, Mary Morton. *Timberrr . . . A History of Logging in New England*. Danbury, CT: Millbrook Press, 2003.

Desjardin, Thomas A. *"Stand Firm Ye Boys from Maine": The 20th Maine of the Gettysburg Campaign*. Gettysburg, PA: Thomas Publications, 1995.

Egan, Joseph, and Donn Fendler. *Lost on a Mountain in Maine*. New York, NY: Harper Trophy, reprint, 1992.

Goodridge, Harry, and Lew Dietz. *A Seal Called Andre*. Camden, ME: Down East Books, 1975.

Hunter, Julia A., and Earle G. Shettleworth Jr. *Fly Rod Crosby: The Woman Who Marketed Maine*. Gardiner, ME: Tilbury House, 2000.

Leamon, James S. *Revolution Downeast: The War for American Independence in Maine*. Amherst: University of Massachusetts Press, 1993.

Lemke, William. *The Wild, Wild East: Unusual Tales of Maine History*. Camden, ME: Yankee, 1989.

McBride, Bunny, and Eunice Nelson-Bauman. *Molly Spotted Elk: A Penobscot in Paris*. University of Oklahoma Press, 1997.

O'Toole, James M. *Passing for White: Race, Religion, and the Healy Family 1820–1920*. Amherst, MA: University of Massachusetts Press, 2002.

Rich, Louise Dickinson. *The Coast of Maine: An Informal History and Guide*. New York: Crowell, 1956.

Rolde, Neil. *The Baxters of Maine: Downeast Visionaries*. Gardiner, ME: Tilbury House, 1997.

———. *The Interrupted Forest: A History of Maine's Wildlands*. Gardiner, ME: Tilbury House, 2003.

———. *Maine: A Narrative History*. Gardiner, ME: Harpswell Press, 1990.

Roop, Connie, Peter Geiger Roop and Peter E. Hanson. [Illustrator]. *Keep the Lights Burning, Abbie*. Minneapolis, MN: Carolrhoda Books, reprint, 1987.

Smith, Mason Phillip. *Confederates Downeast: Confederate Operations In and Around Maine*. Portland, ME: Provincial Press, 1985.

Taylor, Alan. *Liberty Men and Great Proprietors: The Revolutionary Settlement on the Maine Frontier, 1760–1820*. Chapel Hill: Published for the Institute of Early American History and Culture, Williamsburg, Virginia, by University of North Carolina Press, 1990.

Description and Folklore

Blagdon, Tom, Jr. *First Light: Acadia National Park and Maine's Mount Desert Island*. Englewood, CO: Westcliffe Publishers, 2003.

Gould, John. *There Goes Maine: A Somewhat History, Sort of, of the Pine Tree State*. New York: Norton, 1990.

Heinrich, Bernd. *A Year in the Maine Woods*. Reading, MA: Addison-Wesley, 1994.

Ives, Edward D. *George Magoon and the Down East Game War: History, Folklore, and the Law*. Urbana: University of Illinois Press, 1988.

Sample, Tim, and Steve Bither. *Maine Curiosities: Quirky Characters, Roadside Oddities, and Other Offbeat Stuff*. Guilford, CT: Globe Pequot Press, 2002.

Anthologies

Austin, Phyllis, Dean Bennett, and Robert Kimber, eds. *On Wilderness: Voices from Maine*. Gardiner, ME: Tilbury House, 2003.

Fischer, Jeff. *Maine Speaks: An Anthology of Maine Literature*. Brunswick, ME: Maine Writers and Publishers Alliance, 1989.

Phippen, Sanford, Charles Waugh, and Martin Greenberg, eds. *The Best Maine Stories: A Century of Short Fiction*. Camden, ME: Down East Books, 1986.

Shain, Charles, and Samuella Shain, eds. *The Maine Reader/ The Down East Experience 1614 to the Present*. Boston: David R. Godine, 1997.

Sprague, Laura Fecych, ed. *The Mirror of Maine: One Hundred Distinguished Books that Reveal the History of the State and Life of its People.* Orono and Portland: University of Maine Press and Baxter Society in Association with the Maine Historical Society, 2000.

Index

Acton, 66
Addie, Johnny, 95–96
Ali, Muhammad, 93–98
Andover, 30
Andre, 103–8
Andropov, Yuri, 109, 110
Annan, Kofi, 126
Aroostook, 23–24, 26–27, 61, 82
Asleh, Asel, 127–31
Augusta, 25, 27, 72

Bailey & Company's Circus, 51, 59
Bailey, Dr. Gamaliel, 43–44
Bangor, 26, 37
Bangor and Aroostook Railroad, 82
Bangor Whig, 26
Bates, Helen, 72
Baxter, Percival, 73, 134
Bellamy, "Black Sam", 133
Blyth, Samuel, 18–19, 21–22
Boon Island, 8, 11
Boxer, 18–22
Bradford, 35
Bradley, Arthur, 88, 89
Brain, Dr. Jeffrey, 5
Breeches Buoy, 89–90
Breeze, John, 122, 123, 124
Brennan, Joseph E., 104–7
Bryant Pond, 115–20
Bulmer, Allen, 78–79
Burgess, Abbie, 46–50
Burgess, Samuel, 46–47, 49
Burrows, William, 18–19, 21–22

Caribou, 62–64
Cavalcante, Bernard, 125
Chandler's River, 13, 14
Chickering, Sabin, 58–59
Clara, 51
Clay, Cassius, 93–98
Coolidge, Calvin, 76
Cox, James M., 76
Crosby, Cornelia "Fly Rod", 61–65
Cumings, D. L., 62–63
Curtis, John Bacon, 35–40
Curtis & Son, 36–38

Davies, Robert, 3
Davis, Oscar, 122
Dawes, Carlton, 100
Day, Elizabeth, 56
Deane, John, 7, 8, 10, 11, 12
Digby, Mr., 3
Dinsmore, G. M., 51
Dixville Notch, 30–31
Downeast, 102
Drinkwater, Earle, 89–90

Eddy, Mary Baker, 134
Early, Patricia, 117–18
Eastern Argus, 19, 20–21
Easton, 83
Electrolytic Marine Salts Company
    (EMS Co.), 66–69, 71
England, Gordon, 125
Enterprise, 18–22

Fairfield, John, 24, 25, 26
Fendler, Donn, 77–81
Field & Stream, 64
Fisher, Charles E., 66–70
Fletcher, Hurley, 101–2
Fort Fairfield, 24
Fort Saint George, 2–6
Foster, Benjamin, 14, 16
Frane, Cletus, 122–23
Fromsdorf, Helmut von, 125
Frost, Robert, 39

George II (king of England), 28
Gift of God, 1, 4
Gilbert, Raleigh, 3, 4–5
Goodridge, Harry, 103–4, 106–7
Gottschalk, Bobbie, 126–28, 130
Grand Trunk Railway, 33
Grant, Abbie. *See* Burgess, Abbie
Grant, Isaac, 49
Grant, John, 49

Hampden, 35
Harding, Warren G., 76
Harper's Weekly, 55
Hartford Courant, 69
Harvey, John, 25
Hathaway, Elden, 115–20
Hobbs, Annie Bell, 8
Hodges, Russ, 96–97
Houlton, 82–83, 85
Huckleberry Finn, 39
Hull, Isaac, 19
Hunt, John, 3, 4, 5

Illustrated Newspaper, 55

James I (king of England), 1
Jeregan, Prescott F., 66–70
Jaronik, Daniel, 122, 123
Johnson, Alice, 116–17, 118
Johnson, Charles, 53
Jones, Ichabod, 13
Jonesboro. *See* Chandler's River

Journey to the Soviet Union,
  109, 113

Katahdin, Mount, 77, 79, 80
Kennebec River, 6, 99–100, 102
Kennebago Lake, 61
Kennebeck Spruce Gum
  Company, 39
Kent, Edward, 23
Kittery, 28, 134
Kulagin, Vladimir, 113–14

Ladd, William, 134
Langman, Christopher, 7, 9, 10,
  11, 12
Larrabee, Richard, 69
Lawton, Paul, 125
Lewis, Raymond, 87–91
Lewiston, 54, 93–98
Lime Street, 113
Lincoln, Abraham, 44
Liston, Sonny, 93–98
Lockhart, William, 88
Longfellow, Henry Wadsworth, 55
Lost on a Mountain in Maine, 81
Lubec, 67–68, 71
Lubec Herald, 68
Luttrell, John, 121–24
Luttrell, Lorraine, 121, 124

Machias, 13–17
Madrid, 66
Maine Sunday Telegram, 108
Margaretta, 13–17
Mary and John, 1, 2–3, 4
Masardis, 24, 25, 26
Matinicus Rock, 46
McIntire, Rufus, 24, 25, 26
McLauchlin, James, 24, 25, 26
McLaughlin, "Bull", 102
McMoarn, Nelson, 80–81
Michael, Sam, 93, 94
Milliken, Carl, 73, 74
Monhegan Island, 18

Montreal, Canada, 29
Montreal Board of Trade, 29, 32
Moore, James, 14, 15
Mowatt, Captain, 56
Mussey, John, 22

National Era, 44
Neal, John, 54, 59–60
Nineteenth Amendment to the U. S.
    Constitution, 73, 74, 76
Nottingham Galley, 7, 8, 11, 12
Novadoc, 91

Oakey L. Alexander, 87–92
O'Brien, Jeremiah, 13, 15, 16
Otisfield, 127

Peabody Essex Museum, 5
Peterson, Harold, 122, 123
Phillips, 64
Pinkerton Detective Agency, 70
Pocahontas Steamship Company, 87
Polly, 13, 15
Poor, John, 29–34
Popham (colony), 4–6
Popham, George, 1, 4
Popham, Sir John, 1, 4
Portland, 29, 32–34, 37, 51–60, 75,
    88, 89, 91, 121, 122, 123, 135
Portland Advertiser, 25
Portland Company Works, 33
Portland Evening Express, 72–73, 74
Portland Evening Star, 58
Portland Gazette, 21
Portland Lightship, 91
Portland Press Herald, 105, 108
Portland Transcript, 51, 57, 66, 69,
    70, 71
Portsmouth, New Hampshire, 28
Portsmouth Naval Shipyard, 28
Pravda, 111
Priestas, Joseph, 122

Reed, John H., 94

Revere Journal, 78–79
Richter, Rudi, 85
Riess, Warren, 11
Rogers, David, 90

Saint Dominic's Ice Rink, 93,
    94, 98
Saint John, 24
Saint Lawrence River, 31
Salk, Lee, 113
Scagnelli, Lieutenant J. G. John, 122,
    123, 124
Scott, Winfield, 27
Seeds of Peace, 126–31
Selfridge, 122, 123
Shaw, H. Fenton, 82, 83–87
Skillings, Nancy, 75–76
Skolfield, Alice, 74
Smith, Margaret Chase, 135
Smith, Samantha, 109–14, 130
South Paris, 30
Southard, Gertrude, 74
Southard, William, 74
Square Lake, 61
Stevens, Mayor, 57
Stevenson, Adlai, 106
Stowe, Harriet Beecher, 41–45
Strickland, Hastings, 24, 25
Supreme Court, 28

Thompson, William, 122
Thurlow, Hannah, 56
Tom Sawyer, 38–39
Turner, Levy, 67
Turner, Rodney, 88
Twain, Mark, 38–39
Tyler, Harold, 117

Uncle Tom's Cabin, 44–45
Unity, 13, 15–16
USS *Eagle*, 121–25

Van Buren, 84
Van Buren, Martin, 27

Viles, Bob "Stubb", 100
Violette, Leonard "Buster", 99–102
Virginia, 3–4, 6
Virginia Company of England, 1

Walcott, Jersey Joe, 96–97
Wallach, John, 128, 130, 131
Waterhouse, G. G., 30
Webster–Ashburton Treaty, 27

Webster, Daniel, 23, 27
Westerlund, Ivar, 125
Weston, Hannah and Rebecca, 15, 16
Wiggins, Mr. 57
William (king of the Netherlands), 24
Wilson, Tim, 126, 130
Wisniewski, John, 123

About the Author

Gail Underwood Parker has lived in Cape Elizabeth, Maine, for almost thirty-five years. She is an educator, freelance writer, and author of published articles, columns, and books. She specializes in historical nonfiction and educational materials (history, reading, writing, and music). She is a highly energetic and experienced workshop presenter who enjoys inspiring teachers, students, and parents, giving them immediately usable, down-to-earth techniques for improving home and classroom success.

Ms. Parker has taught music, history, language arts, science, and math. She is also a trained parenting educator, with an emphasis on strategies for children who struggle. She is the proud parent of one adopted, four biological, and four long-term foster children.

Teachers, students, parents, and readers can explore Ms. Parker's new searchable Maine history site, www.historyaliveinme.com, or her author site, gailunderwoodparker.com. She is available as a writer, educator, or visiting author and can be reached by e-mail at gailunderwoodparker@yahoo.com or historyaliveinme@maine.rr.com. She welcomes questions and comments from all readers, especially students.

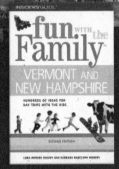

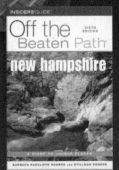